"Sitting Down Was The Tallest I Ever Stood"

From MOB to M.O.G.

"...A raw and stunning read! I am in awe of how God brought the total picture of his circumstances full circle where others can relate and be hungry for real change.

– MICHAEL KROWISZ

"Sitting Down Was The Tallest I Ever Stood"

From MOB to M.O.G.

by Terrance J. Pope

Sitting Down was the Tallest I Ever Stood: From MOB to M.O.G. Copyright © 2022 by Terrance J. Pope All rights reserved.

No part of this publication may be reproduced, stored in a retrieval system, or transmitted in any way by any means, electronic, mechanical, photocopy, recording or otherwise without the prior permission of the author except as provided by USA copyright law.

Published by Terrance Pope is committed to excellence in the publishing industry. The company reflects the philosophy established by the founders.

Published in the United States of America ISBN: 978-1-7338395-4-9

TABLE OF CONTENTS

Dedication   *1*
Foreword   *3*
Book Reviews   *5*
To The Reader   *7*
Introduction   *9*
CHAPTER 1: "There's No Place Like Home"   12
CHAPTER 2: Street Life - Observe and Absorb   22
CHAPTER 3: "The Last Holiday"   53
CHAPTER 4: The Last Run   60
CHAPTER 5: The War Within   72
CHAPTER 6: "God, I surrender"   84
CHAPTER 7: Authentic Manhood   100
CHAPTER 8: "A Step Back to Move Forward"   108
CHAPTER 9: He Who Finds a Wife   114
CHAPTER 10: True Identity   124
CONCLUSION   127
Life Lessons   *133*
Resources   *187*

DEDICATION

I want to dedicate this book to my mother, Lorice Denise Pope. I know that you are always with me, watching and cheering me on. I appreciate you for doing the best that you could to raise my siblings and me. I admire your strength, perseverance, and endurance. But most importantly, your love and time that you gave me. You were the foundation that held our family together. You were our safe haven in times of trouble and our strength in times of weakness. You were not only a mother, but you had become my friend. Although I strayed, your wisdom showed me the road to get back on track. I appreciate, love, and honor you. I dedicate this book to you because you are part of the reason I am who I am today. The good, bad and ugly between us have created something beautiful. Mama, your baby boy inspires now and not discourages. He changes lives and does not cause hindrance, he inspires to heal and not cause harm, but most importantly, he learned to love and not hate. I love you, Mama, and without a doubt, I know you are proud.

FOREWORD

It was January of 2019. I just walked into World Changer Baptist Church located at 8 Mile and Telegraph in Detroit, Michigan for the very first time. I began to hear testimony after testimony of how men's lives had been changed from a life of pain, anger, drug addiction, prison sentences, violence, divorce, and the list went on and on. One of the most impactful testimonies I heard came from a humble man in a wheelchair, Terrance Pope. His testimony was centered around being shot point-blank by a MAC-10 machine gun seven times and being left for dead due to gang life.

Over the next several months, I got to know Terrance on a personal level, and I started to realize that there was something different about him. His testimony of anger, rage, violence, drugs, and street life had changed to a life of love, peace, and forgiveness. As our relationship grew deeper, I began to learn how powerful his testimony was, a testimony that is a light of how Jesus Christ can change someone from the inside out.

In the early part of 2021, Terrance and I started to talk on a regular basis; call it discipleship, mentoring, coaching, or fellowship. I call these meetings a blessing. I knew then that Terrance had a gift that needed to be shared with the world. His gift of public speaking, while being able to make his story impactful and relevant to any audience, is certainly going to change the lives of many and help change the world. It is an honor to not only call Terrance a friend and a brother, but also a passionate, faithful warrior for Jesus Christ.

− PHIL MUNROE

BOOK REVIEWS

This book really brings to life what it was like growing up in a broken home. The details by the author highlight the pain of his childhood and the struggles he endured in order to survive beyond his 18th birthday. A birthday of significance, as his school counselor told him early on in life that he would be dead by 18 if he didn't change his ways. This book is a great story of the redemptive power of Jesus Christ, a powerful story of transformation from gang life to a saved life. A real-life impactful testimony that tells how J Terrance Pope was one way and now he is completely different. A story of what happened in between was Jesus Christ who turned him into a new creation.

— PHIL MUNROE

The book you're holding in your hands is a riveting, real, and powerful testimony of the power of God; to transform an ex-gang member into a humble, bold, and radical follower of "The Way." I highly recommend reading it and buying another copy for any young man struggling to figure life out.

— PASTOR STACEY FOSTER — FORMER SENIOR PASTOR OF LIFE CHANGERS INTERNATIONAL MIN.

The first two chapters of Sitting Down was the Tallest that I Ever Stood is a raw and transparent description of how life in a dysfunctional home can have dangerous consequences. The author's insights can be summarized by the statement, "The Deposit at Home Cashes Out in Society." The description of his home and street life paints a true-to-life picture of the challenges many of our children face today. The author shows unique wisdom in confronting the issues written about.

- PASTOR MIKE KROWISZ

TO THE READER

Dear readers,

Thank you for choosing to read the pages of this book. I wrote this book to inspire, encourage, and remind you that change is possible, and hope is still present. We live in a world where limits are constantly being placed on our capabilities, our future success is measured by our level of education, our body type, finances, our beginnings, the family we were raised in, and more. I am here to eradicate the stigma, and tear down the wall of limitations and say to you, you do not have to be chained to the shackles of conformity or defined by your past. What is seen as an inability is only a chance to reveal God's capability through you.

One of God's greatest gifts to humanity is the gift of choice. We can make the choice to stand out and not fit in. Choose faith and not fear, boldness and not conformity, but most importantly, we can choose to change and not be complacent.

Your parents, teachers, pastors, mentors, and friends may have failed you. Some may even have hurt you. You are not able to change those things, but you are able to change how they affect you and can choose what direction and stance you take. The crushing, the heat, and the cut have made you into a beautiful diamond, and I dare you to shine!

In this book, you'll see the many trials, challenges, and hard decisions I've faced that almost led me one inch from the grave. Statistically, I was supposed to be in prison or dead by 18. But where man sees trash, God sees treasure. And by God's strength, I was able to persevere, overcome, and defy the odds. It is that same victory that I want you to share in.

You were created from a standpoint of victory, destined for greatness and purpose to make an impact, change lives, disturb traditions, and leave a legacy. I pray that you will glean insight, wisdom, and hope from my story that'll help you navigate this life and become all that you are created to be.

"You intended to harm me, but God intended it for good to accomplish what is being done, the saving of many lives."

- Genesis 50:20

INTRODUCTION

It is said that before someone dies, their life flashes before their eyes in a split second. Since I was a child, I've always wondered what a man's last images, words, or last thoughts were before he took his last breath. Was he afraid, or was he like the tough guy in a gangster movie who says, "Take me, I'm ready to die?"

There were even times I played out my death in my head. I imagined myself going out like Nino Brown, with an automatic weapon, shooting at everyone who opposed me, with a cigarette hanging halfway out of my mouth, and my last words being, "I'm going out just like I came in, gangster." I even imagined my funeral, all my homies and family members standing over my casket, giving their last remarks, saying how real I was and how I went out like a G.

I never thought about how my death would affect those around me or how it would shatter my mom's heart into a thousand pieces, leave my siblings grieving, or worst, my son without a father and becoming prey to the vultures. I guess I was always more focused on the accolades of the world instead of the legacy of my family.

TV, music, and whatever we are subjected to in the environments we find ourselves, have a way of creating a utopia, but life has a funny way of showing us that our imagination serves us. Reality has its own rules. In the words of the wisest man who ever walked this earth, "The heart of man plans his way, but the Lord establishes his steps" (Proverbs 16:9).

"You may not like the soil that you were planted in but there will come a time for you to choose how you grow."

– TERRANCE J POPE

CHAPTER 1

"There's No Place Like Home"

It was in the late hours when a loud scream and a thump from downstairs shook me out of my sleep. My heart was pounding, it felt as though it was trying to escape from my chest. I heard the scream again, and glass shattering from downstairs, and this time I recognized the voice. It was my mother yelling, followed by the words, "Call the police."

I jumped up in a panic, rushing downstairs to save my mom from the villain that had entered our home. Once I got to the bottom of the wooden stairs and stared through the gap of the banister, I saw that the villain was once again my dad. Balling up his tongue, his eyes bloodshot red from too many beers, he charged at my mother like a wild bull.

My two sisters, older brother, and I stood on the stairs in panic and fear, crying and screaming, "Dad, please stop!"

I remember as we stared at each other's feet as they moved back and forth, as if we were playing a game of who would intervene first. I looked up at my oldest brother, hoping that he would take the lead, but he looked just as afraid as me because we knew that if we tried to help, our punishment would be even greater.

As we sat there and watched him fight my mother, my eyes fixed on my dad like a nuclear ready to launch. Tears flowed hastily down my face, my nails dug into the palms of my hand, and my blood began to rush to the top of my head. The repeated thoughts going through my six-year-old mind were, "I wish I was big enough so I can kill him."

Abuse was constant in my home, be it verbally or physically. No one was safe; we were all being broken in our own way. My parents created a culture and not too soon after, my siblings and I adopted it. My oldest brother, Ernest, would beat me up, and my little sister, Latrice, and I would fight all the time. Nobody really messed with Britney. She was the quiet one, the straight-A student. We called her Mama's favorite. But she could have a mean steak at times. I remember watching her grab a girl by the hair and spun her around twice, then threw her into the wall. She even beat me up once after I irritated her for almost 20 minutes.

My siblings and I loved each other, but we just didn't know how to love each other. We had no example of conflict resolution, and we had never seen what a healthy relationship looked like; we only mimicked what we saw. See, my parents were the 'do as I say and not as I do' type. My dad would say, "Learn how to walk away from a fight," but later that night, he showed no restraint in fighting my mom or choking me until I passed out on the kitchen floor. Or my mom would say to my siblings and me, "Don't call each other out your name," but later she'd be calling us everything but children of God.

The difference between my mother and father was my mother used to have this measure of guilt in her face when she had offended one of us. I could easily see that Mom was sorry, although pride would never let her say it. A simple, "Do y'all want to go to McDonald's today?" was her way of apologizing.

Now, don't get me wrong, if I had the choice to choose my mom all over again, I would. Aside from a few flaws, she was great. She worked hard to keep a roof over our heads and food on our table. We didn't have much, but she knew how to make a little look good. She not only cared for us, but also for her nieces and nephews. Our house was their safe house, and she was most of her nieces and nephews' favorite aunt. One thing was for certain: we knew Mama had our back. We might have scratched the surface sometimes, but she would never let us fall. We might have questioned her methods of discipline, but we never questioned her love for us.

My dad, when sober, had his perks too, but his anger always overrode any wisdom and logical thinking. He was a great provider, a hard worker, and he kept us clothed. He even tried doing fatherly activities, but even that failed. He had taken my brother and me to work with him once or twice. I was excited at first, but eventually, I hated going, because EVERY TIME I made a mistake with hammering a nail, or was afraid to climb the ladder and get on the roof, he'd curse at me and call me a soft a** B**** or stupid. I felt so low and insufficient that I began to think to myself that I could never do anything right.

I remember once when my father cursed at me, my older brother looked at me as if he could feel the emotion of pain oozing from my soul. As I sat with my head down, struggling to fight back my tears, my brother came over and grabbed my right hand, placing it on the hammer with his hand over mine and began to show me how to hammer properly. I wiped the tear from my left eye and began trying again.

My dad also tried celebrating with me when I got my first good report card. One evening, my mom came in from work, with the biggest smile on her face. She reached into her purse, pulled out an envelope, and handed it to my dad. As he read it, he shook his head in approval. He sat me on his lap and said, "Good job." It was the first time I remember him saying anything good about me, and then the craziest thing happened. He popped off the top of his beer and placed it up to my mouth and said, "Drink, you're a man today." I was a 7-year-old kid, and I was so confused about what was happening.

I remember thinking to myself, *Does this really make me a man?* I refused at first, out of being uncomfortable and not knowing whether he was joking or not. But he insisted. I grabbed the bottle, held my breath, and started drinking. I remember saying, "This tastes like throw up (vomit)," while coughing, spitting, and wiping my mouth.

He only reply was, "This will get some hair on your chest."

We would also have movie night at the drive-in on the weekends. My siblings and I used to love movie night. The buttery popcorn and the sour patch candy were my favorite. But it seemed like every time we left, my mother and father would argue because he had one too many beers.

One time, my siblings and I were in the back of my dad's van sleeping. We had just left the movies when we were startled out of our sleep by the aggression and loud tone of my dad's voice. When I looked up, he was speeding and yelling at my mom, making threats to crash the van. He would speed and then come to a quick halt, causing the tires to screech. He then started doing a full 360 in the middle of a road. He did that to create fear in my mom, but he didn't consider that his children were in the back being tossed and turned like a salad. Crying and afraid for our lives. My dad had good intentions, but very poor communication skills, serious anger issues, and a lack of self-control. And because of this, his efforts were always in vain.

Parental Advisory

"Children are like sponges; what they are exposed to, they quickly absorb, cognitively premature to decipher right from wrong, good from bad, until a consequence or correction follows."

TERRANCE J. POPE

In my home, as a child, we were taught the basics of do's and don'ts, like respect our elders, don't curse, don't talk back, pay attention in school, don't get in trouble. I can see that my parents tried their best to equip us for this world. I still hold true to those principles to this day. But as they did their best to advise, they failed at applying parental discretion.

Everything that we watched, listened to, and entertained in our home contradicted everything that we were being taught and began slowly shaping my world without my consent. I began to think about sex, gang banging, and smoking my first joint before I could even spell my name correctly. At seven years old, I was sitting in a precinct, potentially being charged with sexual assault. By age 11, I was in juvenile detention for arson, and was having sex by 12.

I don't blame my parents for not knowing better, well, not anymore. As I got older, I finally understood that they were never taught the dangers of *indecent exposure*, at least in this regard. And that what we expose ourselves to will shape our very existence; it's where evil desires are awakened, perspectives are created, and habits are born. And what goes unchecked, we inevitably subject our children to, and the cycle repeats itself.

We've all probably heard or even quoted these words: "You are what you eat." Proverbs 23:7 says, "So a man thinks so is he." It is the principle that what we entertain in our minds becomes the driving force for our character. I would later come to the complete revelation of this truth. My life would go on autopilot, driven by the subconscious, leading me to a place of no return.

The Deposit at Home Cashes Out in Society

I sat there in the principal's office with my head down, afraid, nervously swinging my legs and rubbing my thighs while listening to him tell my mother about my poor behavior and anger issues. He suggested that I see the school counselor, advising that I'd be repeating first grade and placed in their special education program. He went as far as telling her that I would be in prison or dead by the age of 18 if my behavior continued. Boy, how I regretted bringing that dead bird to school and putting it in my teacher's chair as a prank. I just knew when we got home and my mother told my father that that would be my last day on earth.

When we got home, my mother was reluctant to tell my father what had happened. I believe she was more afraid than me. She ended up telling him that I was failing first grade and that I would be placed in special education, but she omitted the rest to spare me a beating. But my dad had already been drinking and what seemed small to my mom was a huge deal to my dad. He began to take off his leather belt and told me to pull my pants down and take off my shirt. I looked over at my mom, waiting for her to say something, anything that would save me, but she just stared at me with a look of regret, as if she knew she had made a mistake. He Began beating me until welts were all over my back and behind, and blood was leaking from my wounds. I was bruised so badly that my mom called the school the following day to tell them I wouldn't be coming in because I was sick.

After the beating, I hurried to my room, slammed the door, and put my face in the pillow, screaming as loud as I could. I had wished I was dead many times, but this was different. I meant it.

In retrospect, my parents were always punishing me for mimicking them. I mean, no excuses; wrong is wrong, and the following should be a consequence. But I was only cashing out what they'd deposited. A public manifestation of our home acculturation. I was never taught how to properly express myself or how to put my emotions in check. With everything that was going on at home, being bullied in school and by some of my family members, and being treated like an outcast by my peers in my neighborhood, I had only one counteracting tool: aggression.

Between the tension in the office, the disappointment on my mother's face, and the stern stare from my principal when he asked, "Terrance, what's going on?" I didn't know what to do. I knew how I felt in that office that day; I just didn't know how to express it.

Everything seemed so tangled up and complex in my head when I went to explain myself, and the only thing that would come from my mouth was, "Uh, uh I don't know." If only I could have simplified things and responded, "I'm sad, afraid, I don't feel loved or feel like I fit in anywhere, and I'm lonely," just maybe, my life could have turned out differently, because that day wouldn't be the end of my troubles. In fact, I believe that day was the beginning of a life that would lead me one inch from the grave.

Reflective Thought: *Failing to equip children with the necessary tools that are needed to have a mentally and emotionally balanced life, like how to respond, manage their emotions, affirmation, and exaltation, typically and almost inevitably results in uncontrolled anger, identity crisis, and low self-esteem. As a result, they become enslaved to the world's view of them, yearning to fit in and willing to compromise.*

"When we are born, we are a reflection of our parents, but when we die, we are a reflection of the decisions that we made."

– Unknown

CHAPTER 2

Street Life - Observe and Absorb

My dad went to jail when I was nine years old. I can't say at that time I was bothered. Truthfully, I was kind of relieved. I'm sure my mom was too. She had recently prayed that God would give her the strength to walk away from their relationship, and God was about to answer her prayers in an unexpected way. I can remember that night like it was yesterday.

We were at my grandmother's house. It was our second night staying at her house because two days prior, my mom and dad had gotten into another huge fight, and my mother finally got tired and built up the courage to leave. It was around midnight, and my siblings and I were sleeping on the living room floor, bunched up like newborn puppies to keep warm from the cool breeze that seeped under the door from outside, when my dad came beating on the door, yelling my mother's name. I jumped out of my sleep, startled and confused while my siblings were trying to figure out what was going on. I took the opportunity to try and cover up my pee spot.

My mom opened the door and my dad had this look on his face, as if he had seen a ghost. He was speaking so fast that I could barely make out what he was saying. All I remember hearing him say was, "Police." My mom grabbed her jacket and told us to lock up and left hastily with him.

That would be the last time we saw our dad for a while. He would spend the next nine years incarcerated. We stayed with my grandma for a short while after that, until my mom found a place right down the street. We were already familiar with the neighborhood and knew most of the people because we spent most of our childhood at my grandmother's house. It is the neighborhood where most of my family is from and where I was introduced to the hood gang, the 3rd Street Boys.

In my hood, you had the triple OG's, the OG's, and then there was my brother's generation. My brother and his friends were my first real exposure to gang life. I mean, they were literally acting like the men in the movies I'd watched. They had parties, the girls, guns, drugs, and beef (a hood term for having problems with another gang). I would sit there and listen to them as they laughed and talked about the fights they were in with their rivals and the fun they had with the girls the night before as they sat smoking their weed and talking. I was sitting there soaking it all in, imagining myself being at those events.

Although everything sounded exciting, I also saw the danger that lifestyle brought with it, when my brother stumbled into my grandmother's house with blood all over his face and shirt, nearly beaten half to death by his enemies. Or hearing that one of their rivals was just murdered right around the corner from our home. For some reason, that didn't stop me from wanting that life. Maybe it was the glory, the respect, and having people fear me that was so appealing to an insecure kid, who always felt rejected and worthless by his peers and family members.

I remember I used to dream of being a Martin Luther King, or wanting to be a cop, a fireman, or an actor. I used to want to change the world and be a hero for the helpless. As a child, I would wrap a pillowcase around my neck and pretend to be a superhero saving the world from the bad guys. But those dreams faded, as life was slowly beat the hope out of me. And all I wanted to be now was a 3rd Street boy.

Almost everyone in my neighborhood was rapping it, from the girls to the boys, young and old. It was spray-painted everywhere: on the stores, the street signs, and the sidewalk. They wore it on their shirts and had it tattooed on their bodies. I would walk to the corner store and see a gang of guys standing in front of it, including some of my older cousins, smoking weed, talking loudly, playing loud music, and drinking. I used to be in awe of their cars, with their colorful paint jobs, how they were lifted up with shiny big rims, and the sound system that shook their trunks, as if a gorilla was trapped inside. As I walked through the crowd, some would give me a high five, and others would horseplay with me. They even gave me my first nickname (Juice) because they said I resembled the chubby kid who acted in the movie Lean on Me.

One day, heading back from the store, one of my cousin's friends looked at me and said, "What's up, Little 3rd Street?" His name was P-Nut, at least, that's what we called him. He was one of the coolest guys I ever met. He wore this orange and black jacket that I just thought was the coolest. He had a smooth walk and the talk to match; everyone loved and respected him. Sadly, he was shot and killed in front of that same store a few months later.

When he called me Little 3rd Street, I remember smiling so big inside while trying to keep a straight face and putting a little base in my voice to sound older when I replied, "What's up OG?" That day, it was official. He certified me as a 3rd Street boy. I thought I would have to get jumped in like I saw in movies, but hey, if he said I was 3rd Street, then that's what it was. I began rapping 3rd street everywhere I went: in school, at the rec center, and even in church. I wrote it on all my notebooks and drew it on my arm and shirts with markers. For the first time in my short 11 years of life, I finally felt like I belonged.

I remember getting into trouble in the fifth grade for telling a classmate that I was in a gang called the 3rd Street Boys. He ended up telling the teacher, and the principal called my mom. Her belt met my behind. My mom was not having it! She tried her best to keep my brother and me from getting involved in the streets. She threatened to take us to juvenile detention many times, called our uncles and older cousins to discipline us, and even whooped us with broomsticks or whatever else she could get her hands on. But my brother and I had already observed and absorbed so much, on top of having our only example of a man being a man who had no idea of what a man was. Then he went to prison and we were left without any male guidance. We had only the guys in our neighborhood to show us what manhood was, and that included my uncles and older guy cousins, and they were all gang members and drug dealers too.

Now, I'm not saying that we couldn't have turned out differently or made better decisions, but given our situation, our chances were slim. We were a product of our environment. And as far as my brother and I were concerned, we were doing what real men do. My brother had already started selling drugs by age 16. I was 11 years old at the time and was following in his footsteps not too long after.

At that exact age, I got my first real taste of being incarcerated. After coming home from Coney Island one early morning with my older brother, two cop cars were sitting outside of my home. As I laid my bike down on my front lawn, the officers got out and started to approach me with their handcuffs in hand. I remember looking over at my mom as she stared back at me in disappointment. I was so confused and afraid, not understanding what was happening. I figured it was because of me constantly getting suspended from school and my mother finally having enough. I immediately began to cry and even considered running, but for a chunky kid, I knew I wouldn't get far. I had completely forgotten that two days before, I had set the garage and house hallway of the boy down the street on fire. And now my bad decision had come to meet its consequence.

While in juvenile detention, I had a lot of time to reflect and think about my future. How I wanted to do better. I spent a lot of my time reading and praying to ease the pain and escape my reality. I cried almost every night and I couldn't eat for a week. I missed my freedom and I just wanted to go home. I made a lot of promises to my mom and the judge to change my ways while sitting in that courtroom crying. I was really sincere with my statement because, honestly, I really wanted to be better. That good kid was still in me. I just didn't know how to be better and had no one to model it for me.

I always knew I was different from most kids. My idols were Martin Luther King, Malcolm X, and Tupac. Their revolutionary spirit, and their ability to speak with such conviction and authority had always captivated me. When I was just seven years old, I used to practice speaking to an audience about change in the bathroom. I imagined myself standing on a stage, speaking to thousands of people, telling them how they should be good and not bad, and to listen to their parents. I laugh about it now because I was only repeating to my imaginary crowd, the things that the adults told me. I dreamed of being a public figure, someone that people could look to for hope, but I had no one to affirm and invest in that side of me because it wasn't popular where I came from. You had to be a gangster to earn any respect, so my aspirations were slowly drowned out by my environment, and it felt like I had no choice but to conform to the mediocrity around me.

A month later, I was released from juvenile detention and was back home under the same influence. I was back to my same routine. Since that time, I've always been fearful of prison. I hated being confined to a facility and under the authority of someone, and I hated being away from family. I knew for certain that it was a place that I never wanted to see again, but as much as I feared it, I feared public opinion more, and if I wasn't a 3rd Street boy, then I would feel like a nobody. And nobody wants to feel like a nobody. So I continued to play with fire, believing I wouldn't get burned again. And the more I got away with things, the more clever and invincible I felt, but the fire was only stalling, warming me up to serve me into the hands of destruction.

"Show me your friends and I'll show you your future."

– UNKNOWN

Reflective Thought:: We all may have heard the saying, "If you hang with four bums, you'll become the fifth one." Who we are surrounded by influences us greatly, and it does it without our consent. We become like sponges on the shores of the sea, soaking up every tide we are exposed to. It shapes our very existence, our perspective, communication, understanding, and heart's stance. We become enslaved to public opinion and shackled by fear. We must build our circle around people and places that are conducive to positive growth. People who encourage our transformation and invest in our gifts.

Jumping Off the Porch

It was my second week of middle school, and I thought I would make it my business to let everyone know that I was a 3rd Street boy. I thought it would make me popular, stand out, or better yet, make people fear me, but to my surprise, it did quite the opposite. It did make people notice me since I was acting like the new big bad wolf on campus, but I wasn't noticed in the way I had expected. I became a target and prey to the residing wolf pack, the 12th Street Boys, and what made it worse was that my new school was on their turf.

One afternoon, coming from lunch period, I was walking up to the second-floor heading to class, when I was approached by over seven guys. At that moment, I knew I'd done something wrong, but in my ignorance, I had no idea what it was until one of the guys said, "No other gangs are welcome in our school if we don't give them a pass." He was the biggest guy out of the group and looked as if he had failed eight grade a few times.

I knew I didn't stand a chance against this guy, so I said, "Ok," and tried walking off. He then grabbed me by the shirt and slammed me to the ground while the other guys punched and kicked me. I would like to tell you that I got up, dusted my shoulders off, and was ready to go for round two, but the truth is, I was afraid, more afraid than I'd ever been. I mean, I'd gotten into small fights in the neighborhood, but it was nothing like this. I had never been jumped by a gang before, and I didn't know how to process or react to what had happened. All I knew was I felt vulnerable, confused, and afraid. I didn't say anything to my teachers because I knew it would only make my situation with those guys worst, especially after they threatened me with "snitches get stitches" after they jumped me.

After school, I snuck out through the back door and ran home, leaving my sister to walk home by herself. I did that for a couple of weeks before my mom caught on and asked me why I was making it home from school before my sister then said not to let it happen again. I still kept quiet about what had happened. I couldn't tell her or my older brother about what was going on at school because I didn't want my mom to overreact or my older brother and little sister to make fun of me.

One night before school, I sat in the basement thinking about how I was going to handle these guys. I remember thinking to myself, *I'm tired of running and being afraid.* I then remembered that my mom's boyfriend at the time stashed his gun in the basement. I knew where it was because I snuck in and played with it once or twice before. I went to see if it was still stashed in the top cabinet right behind the bar. I opened up the cabinet and there it was, all black with a box of bullets beside it. The next morning, I got up for school battling with myself, trying to decide if I should take the gun to school or not. Within minutes of having to leave for school, I'd finally built up the courage to grab it and stick it down in the bottom of my backpack, putting my shirt over it.

I never really planned on shooting anyone. I didn't know if I could or if I wanted to. I just wanted to scare the guys and to prove to myself that I wasn't the punk that I was feeling like. While on the playground, feeling the excitement of bringing a gun to school, I decided to show it to a couple of guys to redeem myself after everyone heard about what had happened to me on those stairs that afternoon. After recess, we headed back to class. By the time I was able to completely sit down in my seat, the police were swarming my classroom. When the officer approached my desk and asked me to step out of the class, it hit me that someone had ratted me out. After searching me and my locker and not finding anything, they finally released me back to class. I had already stashed the gun behind the bushes on the playground, planning to go back for it after school. Thank God I did, I almost peed my pants getting searched by the police. I for sure would have pooped being handcuffed and put in the back of their car.

The principal called my mom and let her know what had happened. My mom believed I was telling the truth when I told her that my peers were lying, but my deceptiveness didn't bypass my brother. He had already discovered that the gun was missing earlier that day. I ended up telling him the truth about what was going on, and the next day he and his friend were at my school, waiting for me to come out, to point out the guys that had been bullying me. Let's just say I never had to deal with those guys again.

The word traveled fast through the school that I had brought a gun to school. I was eventually kicked out of the school because of it. But before that decision was finalized, I started to notice a level of respect from the guys that jumped me and even some of the guys in my class. Kahlil who is one of my best friends until this day came over to my desk and asked me if I really had a gun. He asked if I remembered him which I did not at the time. Then he reminded me that he and I had a fight in elementary school, and I punched him in the stomach and pulled down his pants. I didn't realize he was that scrawny kid I did that to since he had grown to what seemed to be 5 inches taller than me and was built like an action figure.

About a few weeks later, another classmate came into the class named Zaret. He talked a lot, mainly about how crazy his former school was and how good he was at fighting. We became close friends as well, but were always in competition. We argued about who was the best fighter, who got more girls, and even who would shoot someone first. It seemed like the only thing we could agree on was that we loved each other and we had each other's backs.

Later, they would introduce me to Henry, who we called Hen for short. He was the quiet type, but you know how the saying goes, "Don't mistake quietness for weakness." I found that out the hard way with Hen after testing him and getting grabbed and slammed on my back. That guy was strong as an ox and he didn't take crap from anyone.

Then there was Brandon. We called him Beazy. He and I had a rough start. We knew each other from the neighborhood. He used to bully me when I had just moved to the neighborhood, until one day, I grabbed my dog and my bat and stood my ground. He was two years older than me, with a full red beard, and wondered why I would run when he asked if I wanted to fight? I wouldn't say he became scared of me, but he definitely started to respect me and I respected him because he not only talked a good game, but he was able to back it up as well.

We found out that we all had similar backgrounds, struggles, and wounds, and we were all from the same hood. I believe we were all drawn to each other because of our desire to belong; we were all the black sheep of our families. We were looked down on, talked about, and doubted throughout our whole lives. So we all had something to prove. And that was my crew. The new generation of the 3rd Street Boys. Just five kids trying to find our place in this world.

Now, of course, we had other friends in the hood, but our bond was different and stronger. We were more like brothers and everyone knew it. If you crossed one of us, you crossed all of us.

We were five kids who thought we were ready for a grown man's game. We were all just jumping off the porch. (Jumping off the porch is a term we use in the streets when someone goes from watching street activity to being involved in street activity themselves.)

We started out doing small criminal acts such as jumping other guys, stealing from stores, breaking and entering (B&E), stealing bikes, and snatching purses to get our feet wet. As we got older and got away with things, the more chances we took, one of those being, we began stealing cars. Hen was the mastermind behind our car thefts. He taught us all how to steal a car including me, who was only 13 at the time and didn't know how to drive yet. He would steal a car, then take us to go steal another car, then have me drive it back to the neighborhood. It was a crazy and dangerous tactic, but it worked. I was driving like I'd done it my whole life.

I can't count how many high-speed chases we got into and near-death experiences. From someone catching us stealing their car and shooting at us to fleeing from the police in a ram truck going the opposite way on the freeway. We even had some homies get shot while caught stealing a car. Hen was even hit in the head with a pole after being caught stealing a car. The crazy part was, whilst all my boys had been caught by the police, I'd never been. They used to jokingly call me an informant because they couldn't understand how the biggest, the slowest, and wildest one of the crew constantly got away. I used to joke back and say, "Because I'm the clever one."

Truthfully, there was only one real explanation. I didn't know it at the time, but as I got older, I realized that God's grace was with me. I should have realized it the day we got into a high-speed chase and I was so terrified that I began to pray, and when my friends jumped out and ran, I stayed inside the car. I was certain I had been caught, but when I finally stuck my head up from the back seat to look out the rear window, all five police cars' doors were open and their cars were empty. They had gone after my friends, leaving me to just step out of the vehicle and walk right up to a female friend's apartment. Or even the time when I was standing on the corner and some guys did a drive-by and the bullet whistled past my ear, missing me by an inch.

One thing I've always known how to do was pray when faced with difficulties. It was the only thing that ever brought me peace. I can't remember exactly where I picked it up or at what age, maybe it was from the neighborhood bible study my siblings and I attended as kids or the Sunday service my mom dragged us to. But it has always been a big part of my life for as long as I can remember. But I couldn't tell them that the wildest guy out of the crew prayed; they would have clowned me for years.

Around this time, my older brother was serving a four-year sentence in Ohio because of a drug charge, and my mom had no idea what I was up to, besides the people in the neighborhood calling her to tell her about my mischievous acts. But because there wasn't any proof, my mom never knew who to believe. With a father and brother in prison and a mother who was slowly losing her grip on me, I felt as though I was finally the captain of my ship and that I was officially a man.

The evolution continued; we went from not only stealing cars to also selling drugs and armed robberies. We were on a fast train to destruction and felt untouchable. Most of the guys our age in the neighborhood feared us, and we were demanding respect from the older OG's.

Reflective Thought: *The choices we make today will affect our tomorrow. It may seem innocent and exciting in the beginning, but anything done repetitively creates a habit, and it becomes harder to break over time. When we are moving so fast, we never slow down to see the damage we are causing on the way, and by the time we look back, we are devastated by the trail of fire we left. I encourage you to make calculated decisions, to think 10 steps ahead before making a foolish choice. I was a kid way in over my head,* *being lured in by a false reality and making hasty decisions that would soon cost me way more than I was willing to pay.*

Enemy's Turf

I was 14 years old going into high school, and honestly, I think it was a failure before it even started. For one, I was starting high school as a special ed student. At that time,

we were called the LD kids, which is short for learning disability, and those kids were always made fun of. Secondly, I was going to Northern High School. It was located on the Northend, where the Northend Boys resided, the 3rd Street Boys' long rival gang. The gang that had beaten my brother the day he came running into my grandmother's house.

I have no idea why the beef started or when it did. The crazy part is, we were neighbors. They were located just across our main street, Woodward. It took less than 10 seconds for someone from 3rd Street to step into the Northend territory. That explains why there was so much war; we couldn't help but see each other while going to a gas station or supermarket. I now laugh at how ridiculous it was.

I knew most of the guys already from childhood. We were living on the Northend at the time when my father was still home, but none of that mattered anymore. We were all older, and we no longer saw each other as childhood peers, but instead, enemies. It was a mutual understanding that the 12th Street Boys and 3rd Street Boys would stick together, seeing how the Northend Boys outnumbered us by the hundreds. And you know how the saying goes, "An enemy of my enemy is a friend."

It's crazy how life works sometimes. The same crew that jumped me in middle school was the same crew backing me in high school. But honestly, I trusted no one to have my back like my brothers, and unfortunately, Zaret was the only one who attended the school. Kahlil, Hen, and Beazy were at different schools. So Zaret and I stuck together like glue and were ready for anything that came our way.

The tension was high in school, but everyone sort of kept their distance. There were some guys from each of our hoods who weren't into the whole gang banging thing, which kind of kept the peace between all the gangs. It is kind of hard going after someone's family member or friend when you have developed a level of respect for a person.

I tried going to class and doing the best I could, but their work just seemed a little too challenging. With everything spoken over my life as a kid, I just didn't think I was smart enough to graduate. I had already counted myself out. I knew I only made it to high school because I was in special ed and they passed us along just for coming to class. With everything going on around me, it was a lot harder to focus, especially trying to sneak out of class before the bell rang, so no one would see me leaving out of a special ed class. I skipped school a lot. As soon as my mom would drop me off at the front door, I would head right out the back door, headed to the hood.

And then it happened, the moment of peace ended and the ice was broken between the gangs. One morning while skipping class, I sat on the side of the school stairs talking to a guy I considered a friend, who I would later discover set this incident up. As I sat there, two guys in black hoodies approached me. I knew they were from the Northend because I recognized one of the guys. He was older and around my brother's age, and he had an issue with my brother. Before I could stand and get firm footing, they were already jumping on me. Once finished, they took off running. This was the second time I'd been jumped, and unlike the first time, I stood up and was ready for round two. I was furious!

After that day, everyone from that side became a target. Anyone who even looked like they were from that side had to feel my wrath. Zaret and I were on the hunt for blood throughout the school. When we were spotted together, roaming the halls, everyone knew we were looking for trouble. The rest of the homies would come to the school and beat any Northend guy we could get our hands on and vice versa.

We would have a huge war almost every day after school. I mean, hundreds of teens and adults fighting in the middle of Woodward like we were in a Spartan movie. People were getting stabbed, hit with bottles and bricks, blood was everywhere, traffic backed up, and police and security were all over the place.

By the tenth grade, I was labeled the leader of the 3rd and 12th Street gangs by the police. It wasn't true, but I can see how they would come to that conclusion since I was always heading the after-school wars. But, in my eyes, my homies and I were all equal leaders. They put in just as much work and pulled just as much weight as I did. Everyone in the streets began to call me by my last name, Pope. I was growing into myself. I was a big guy for my age. I had my crew, and I'd made a name for myself, but most importantly, I was respected.

Reflective Thought: *As I stated before, we are often conditioned by the media (television) and our surroundings. We are taught to envy, hate, covet, dehumanize, and degrade one another. We go to war because of jealousy and fight because of hate, with no real explanation to these actions, except greed, pride, and sometimes because it is the thing to do, everyone's doing it.*

I, myself, had no idea why I was at war with the Northend. To this day, there is no clear reason.

James 4:1-2 explains it this way: "Why do you fight and quarrel? It is because your feelings are fighting inside of you. That is why you fight. You want something but you cannot get it. Then you kill. You want something very much and cannot get it. So you quarrel and fight. You do not get it because you do not ask God for it."

In essence, we take because we're empty. We war because we hate ourselves. We fight each other because we fail to win the fight within. But most importantly, we don't know who we are, because we don't know who the creator is.

Leaving the Nest

After so many fights and suspensions and the principal hearing that I shot a gun into a crowd full of people from the Northend, I was expelled from all Detroit Public Schools (DPS). My mom enrolled me in an alternative school. I pretended as if I was leaving out every morning for school, but truthfully, I had already dropped out and the teachers never cared enough to contact my mother to inform her of my absences. I believed she knew but didn't want to accept that her baby boy was heading down the same road as his father and brother. I was spending most of my time in the hood with my homies and my girlfriend at the time, who would later become the mother of my child. I was drinking, smoking, taking pills, gang banging, having sex, and getting into all kinds of trouble.

My mom moved us away from the neighborhood. I think a part of her felt that our move would keep me out of the neighborhood and prevent me from getting into further trouble, especially since the last incident of me coming home covered in blood from being stabbed three times scared her half to death. I was 16 years old and in love and had a strong reputation. I felt that my mom was trying to ruin my life. She would always try to stop me from hanging out with my friends, saying my girlfriend couldn't spend the night with me. She would always yell at me, saying, "Those guys aren't your friends," or "The streets don't love you," and how I was going to end up in prison like my father and brother.

As I look back in retrospect, I understand that she wasn't trying to ruin my life but rather save it. I thought that I knew everything at that time and that my mom didn't know anything. My mom was right, however, I was just blinded by my own desires. I didn't understand it or even want to understand her the night I was sitting in my room at our new home, angry, packing my bags, getting ready to make my great escape. I sat there eagerly waiting for 10:00 pm to strike because I knew that the last Puritan bus stopped running at 10:30. All I could think about was getting back to my girl and the homies; it never crossed my mind that I would break her heart by leaving, or that I'd cause her to stay up all night worrying sick, afraid to answer a late phone call for fear it was someone calling to tell her I'd been killed or locked up. All I was concerned about was finally being free from her authority and doing what I wanted.

At the 10:00 pm strike, I grabbed my two garbage bags full of clothes and headed out the door to my room that led to the backyard.

I took off, running toward the bus stop like a slave to the north. I jumped on the bus, and I was headed to freedom.

Honestly, being on my own was rough. I had already begun to regret my decision to leave when I found myself sleeping in abandoned houses, stolen cars, or having Hen sneak me upstairs in his attic at night so I could sleep. I bounced around a lot, sleeping wherever I could rest my head. I was exhausted from dodging the police that my mom had out looking for me and having no permanent place to go. Seeing my friends and girlfriend going home to their families every night made me miss mine, even my little sister, whom I swore to hate forever. But I'd made my choice. My bed had been made and now it was time to lay in it.

Reflective Thought: *Being stubborn and hasty about leaving home prematurely causes us to have a weak foundation as we develop. When we're hit with life challenges, we become like a collapsing building and a pile of rubbish.*

Our parents may not be perfect, but life has granted them wisdom through experience that can help us navigate this life, saving us from having to make the same mistakes they did. We may feel as though they are out of touch and don't understand us, but as Solomon said in Ecclesiastes 1: 9, "There's nothing new under the sun."

It's funny because I'm a father now, and my son is amazed at how sometimes I can call out an effect even before the cause happens. I explain to him that I'm no prophet, it's simply experience. Times may have changed, but people are still the same. To the young person that might be reading this, try giving your parents a chance to speak; be slow to speak and quick to listen. You might be surprised at what you hear. To the mom or dad reading this, try remembering that you were once a child too. A mutual understanding leads to a common ground.

Like Father Like Son

A year and a half passed after I left home and spoke to my mother. My girlfriend at the time and I got our first place, and we were both so excited. No more sleeping in our car or in a vacant house that her mother had just moved out of recently. She had chosen to stay behind with me when her mom moved out of the neighborhood. We both were willingly homeless in the name of love for some time before finding our first place.

We met in the neighborhood when I was 14 and she was 15. We were two kids in love, at least, that is what we thought. The problem was that I didn't know how to love. We weren't even seven months into our relationship before I started to abuse her verbally and physically. I was a very insecure and broken kid who lacked confidence and was unsure of myself. Although I had earned a tough reputation in the streets, it was only a mask to hide that unconfident and scared little boy. I was never taught how to have a healthy relationship or ever seen one for that matter, so I didn't know how to earn a lady's respect without being dominant. So I did what I knew best and what most insecure men do, and that was to assert my dominance and instill fear in her so that she would never cheat or leave.

Honestly, I was unaware of the tactics I was using then, I was simply mimicking everything I saw growing up and what I'd interpreted as the characteristics of a real man. At that age, it never crossed my mind that I was doing the very thing that I hated my father for. The same hands that I used to hug her with were also used to hit her. The same mouth I used to say I love you with was used to degrade and humiliate her. I was such a walking contradiction and a spitting image of my father. I was surprised she stuck around as long as she did, let alone moved into a place with me.

Us moving into our new home felt like the perfect time to start over. I'd even thought about giving up the street life and started going to church. I just knew I wanted to be better and do things differently, and I couldn't shake the urge to go. For three weeks, I went up to the altar call to say the salvation prayer until, Lisa, the lady who introduced me to Christ as a kid, pulled me to the side and said, "Terrance, you don't have to be saved every week." I had no idea what being saved meant. All I knew was going up there every week felt right. I was searching for something, something bigger than myself. Something better than what I'd always known. I also re-enrolled in school. I knew that it would make my mom proud and maybe restore the hope she once had for me, and if I planned to be successful in life, I knew education was the start.

It was my second day in my GED class, and I sat there listening to the teacher as he taught, and it sounded as if he was speaking another language. It was all jargon to me. After the bell rang to let us out, I approached my teacher's desk and whispered to him, "I'm having a hard time understanding the work."

He loudly replied, "Well, you're in the wrong class because I made it as simple as possible."

I was angry, I slammed the textbook on his desk and headed out. I was embarrassed and discouraged. All of the emotions of that six-year-old kid sitting in the office with his mom and principal had risen once again.

I stormed toward the bus stop while fighting to hold back my tears, never returning to school. I've always felt that I was behind cognitively. I struggled with comprehension. That was part of the reason I'd dropped out of school the first time. I would later learn that it wasn't that I was stupid and couldn't learn, I just learned differently and one style of teaching doesn't fit all. I'm a visual learner, I have to see it in order to process it. Maybe if the teacher had been more educated on the different styles of learning, he would have handled me more gracefully.

I stayed home for a while and gave the streets a break because it was the first time in a long time that I was at peace and I didn't have to watch my back from my enemies or the police. But as time passed, I couldn't resist the pull and the thought that I was missing out on something. I missed the accolades and the respect, the partying, but most importantly, my homies. And before I knew it, I was back in the streets thuggin' as usual. I was back to staying out all hours of the night, and when I did go home, I was drunk and fighting with my girlfriend.

Most of our arguments stemmed from her trying to convince me to leave the streets. She was afraid after the last incident, when some rival gang members caught us walking one night and pulled out a gun, threatening to kill us both. But it seemed the more she tried changing me, the more she sounded like my mother, and the more I felt that she was trying to control my life. Although I knew she was right, I just wasn't ready to admit it. I escaped the truth by responding with aggression, doing drugs, and staying out partying all night or finding another girl who was satisfied with my lifestyle and wouldn't try to force me to change to stay with for a few nights.

She not only reminded me of my mother in her words but also in her endurance and her willingness to stick by my side, regardless of what I put her through. The truth is, I didn't mind being who I was to her because I knew whatever I did or the decisions I made, she would never leave. In the streets, we called women like that "ride or die" chicks. In a sense, it's true, because as she rides, she is dying, dying to her self-respect, true identity in God, her morals, self-esteem, dignity, and good health until she's just simply dead. Just like my father, I was tearing a woman down just to build myself up. But in the end, everyone who exalts themselves will be humbled (Luke 14:11).

> *One's dignity may be assaulted, vandalized and cruelly mocked, but it can never be taken away unless it is surrendered."*
>
> - MICHAEL J. FOX

Reflective Thought: *Why do we reject change? Is it the pain of the stretching? The fear of the unknown? Public opinion or complacency? Dr. Myles Monroe once said, "Change is a gift because it keeps us from living in a permanent state." We know that change is good, but we often reject it, be it creating healthy habits, losing weight, going back to school, or seeking therapy. We choose to stay stagnant, refusing to excel. For me, it was the fear of the growing pains and of the unknown. I knew that changing would be good for me, but I was shackled by bad habits that felt good at the time. I was refusing to change, choosing to live in what could have become a permanent state.*

The Prodigal Son Returns

I was 19 years old and still in the streets selling drugs, having shootouts every other day, and being in high-speed police chases. My brother was in prison serving a 10-year bid, and my father was released after serving nine and a half years in prison and tried to re-establish a relationship with me. There was some good going on around me. My mother and I were back on good terms. I could tell she was happy to have me back around the house, and I was happy to be back around her and my sisters. And I came bearing a gift.

My girlfriend was pregnant with our son. Finally, after years of trying, praying, and having over four miscarriages, it finally happened. Things were going great! My mom was super excited. I enjoyed watching her smile when I gave her the news and how she called all of her friends and sisters to share the news with them.

I finally felt like I'd done something good for her for a change. I'd disappointed her so much in my life, which only brought pain and tears, I was hoping this could make up for things. She was in a good place. She not only got her son back, but she was also getting ready to be a grandma.

Honestly, when I found out I was having a son, it was bittersweet for me. I was happy that I was having him, but I was afraid that I wouldn't know how to love him. I never had a real connection with my dad or any man, so I didn't know how I would be able to connect with my son. I was afraid that I was going to fail him or even not love him enough. I thought that at least if I had a girl, it was a chance I could love her better. Growing up, I'd watched my father cater to my sisters. But I had no idea how to love a son.

We were back and forth staying with my mom and my girlfriend's mom during her pregnancy because we had gotten evicted from our place, and my girlfriend suffered from sickle cell disease, so we thought it would have been better to be around more family in case the pregnancy caused any health problems. We would all take turns keeping an eye on her.

During the time I stayed with my mother, I noticed she had lost a lot of weight but not too much that I felt I needed to be concerned. I just figured she was still grieving the loss of her fiancé. I also noticed her trying to encourage me to stay around the house more, while still respecting that I was a man now. But I didn't think too deeply about it. I just figured she missed her son. But what was to come would shake up my world forever.

Finally, the moment had arrived. On June 11, 2009, my son was born, weighing 6 pounds, 10 ounces. He was a premature baby, born a month before his due date, so they kept him in the intensive care unit for about a week. When I was finally able to hold him in my arms, it seemed as if all my fears had been replaced with a love I'd never experienced before. There was an instant connection, and at that moment, I was ready to give up everything to be everything to my son.

I had no idea how to be a father at twenty years of age or what direction to go. All I knew was that I wanted to be the opposite of what my father was to me. And now that I had my mom on my side, holding and gazing into the eyes of her first grandson, I knew I would succeed. I had finally gotten a glimpse of the way she may have stared at me when I was born, believing in her heart that someday her son would grow to be someone great. Instead, I was a gangster. It was evident I had failed her, and maybe it was too late for me, but it wasn't too late for my son.

CHAPTER 3

"The Last Holiday"

It was only one week away from Thanksgiving when my mom suggested that, instead of doing Thanksgiving the traditional way by going over to a relative's house to spend the holiday with the entire family, we spend it at home with our immediate family, meaning, just her and her children. I thought that it was a little odd that she wanted to do it this way because she was the one who would always drag us over to one of her sister's houses to spend the holiday. Regardless of the fact, it didn't matter much to me. My little sisters and I cracked jokes about the weirdness of it, but we were perfectly fine with the idea.

When we made it to mom's place on Thanksgiving, I could see the joy in her face as she smiled when I walked through the door carrying her grandbaby in his car seat. My sister also had her baby girl, Myair, who she had just two months after my son was born. My mom called them her "two tannies," and she loved them very much. I can still remember the smell of the food when I walked into the house: string beans, yams, greens, turkey, and more! And the old school jams played as she sang and danced. I went into the kitchen to try stealing a piece of cornbread, and she caught me and kicked me out of the kitchen! Man, I was starving and cornbread was her specialty!

I sat there and watched as she smiled, laughed, and played with her grandchildren. She was so happy. Being behind on bills, her car being down, and recently losing her fiancé seemed like it didn't matter at the moment. None of it was going to ruin this moment for her!

My older sister later ended up calling my mom's phone to tell her that she wouldn't be able to make it to dinner. I remember my mom fussing at her over the phone and then hanging up on her. My mom's whole disposition had changed. She was angry, hurt, and soon began to cry. At that time, I was thinking to myself, *Is it that deep?* This wasn't the first holiday that my sister had missed.

My youngest sister and I tried to cheer her up by reminding her that at least we were there. As time passed, my mom relaxed. We sat and ate, but I could still tell that something was bothering her. There was something that she had to get off her chest.

A few days after Thanksgiving, my mom went into the hospital and was admitted. When I went to visit her, she told me that the reason was that her blood pressure was high. This wasn't news to me because my mother had gone into the hospital a few times for high blood pressure, but this time I could sense something was different. I couldn't quite put my hand on it though, but the thought of losing her suddenly made me sick. She came home a few days later, and I later found out that she was never discharged. She decided to leave because Christmas was approaching and she wanted to get back to work to make more money to buy her grandkids some gifts.

It was close to midnight and I was hanging out with friends when the mother of my child called me saying that my mom had just passed out at work and was back in the hospital. When I spoke to my mom that night, she assured me that she was okay and that I didn't have to come up to see her that night as she'd probably be out by morning. I had explained to her that the last bus had already stopped running but that I would be up there to see her first thing in the morning.

I finally made it to the hospital the following day in the afternoon. I walked in and saw my mom laying there, as if she was sleeping with a tube down her throat and nose. It felt like my heart had sunk into my stomach. I walked over and tapped her shoulder and said, "Mom, I'm here." I tried waking her up a few more times, but she did not respond. When the doctor finally came in, I rushed over to her in a panic, asking, "When will my mom be waking up?"

The doctor put her head down and placed her hand on my shoulder. That was when the words that I'd dreaded hearing my entire life rolled out of her mouth. "I'm sorry, we've done all that we could. Your mom won't be waking up. She's dying."

My knees weakened as I stumbled over to the chair, trying to process what I'd just heard. My heart felt like it had just shattered into a million pieces, and my head pounded as I stared at my mother, begging her to wake up. The doctor further began to explain that my mom had been sick for a very long time. That's when it all clicked: the weight loss, the back-and-forth hospital visits, her encouraging me to stay home more, leaving the hospital, and the thanksgiving dinner. My mom knew that she was dying and chose to suffer in silence. That's what she wanted to tell us on Thanksgiving and why she was so angry when my sister couldn't show up.

I blamed myself for missing all the signs. I immediately began to regret running away and putting her through all of that pain. I regretted the time we lost with one another because I was in a hurry to leave home. I regretted breaking her heart. For some reason, I couldn't help but feel responsible for her death, as if my poor life decisions contributed to her death in some kind of way. I was searching for an explanation and needed someone to blame. I blamed the doctors, myself, and also my dad for treating her how he did when we were kids. But the only one to truly blame was my mother. She had refused to take the medication that was prescribed to help her and she had also refused to tell us that she was sick. I don't know her reasons, but regardless of why she chose not to take the medication or tell her children what was going on, it all boils down to one thing, selfishness. My mom had made a poor decision in not communicating with us what was going on, and we were left to deal with the consequences.

As I talked to my mother while she lay there in the ICU, I began to apologize for all I put her through. As I finished talking, a tear had rolled from her right eye down to her cheek. It was clear that she had heard my words. What made things harder was that we had to make the tough decision to pull the plug on her. And that only added more guilt to my conscience. My world was crushed! It felt like I was being pulled into a dark pit with no way to escape.

As I watched my family scream and cry in the waiting room, I sat there in rage. I was mad at myself, my mother, and God. I couldn't bring myself to tears because I didn't cry much. I was always taught that a real man doesn't cry, that we take our hits and keep moving. So that's what I did. I suppressed the tears, but grief has a way of coming out in other ways.

I left that hospital with one mission: to destroy anyone who got in my way, or who had ever crossed me. I was a lion out for blood, and I was determined to get it by any means. I went back to the streets and started terrorizing every place I stepped foot in. I also began to destroy myself even more. I was taking pills, smoking, and drinking more than I ever had. I was trying to escape my reality by staying under the influence of drugs. I even stopped going home to my girlfriend and son for a while. I was barely bathing and eating. I was a complete mess, and I didn't want them to see me that way.

Reflective Thought: *What we conceal cannot be healed. Society encourages us when we're faced with grief or hardships of any kind, to suck it up and to move forward. We quote cliches like, "Only the strong survive," without understanding what real strength is. We interpret suppressing our emotions, pressing forward, and dealing with our problems alone as true strength, and being vulnerable, transparent, trusting, and showing emotions as weakness when it is quite the opposite.*

Suppressing our hurt will only bleed out in other areas of our lives, and we find ourselves bitter, angry, closed off, and hurting everyone we come in contact with. Sickness, anxiety, and depression also start to develop. When we are open about our struggles, hurt, and concerns, it robs anger of its authority and opens us up to a healing process, allowing those broken places to be mended. We begin to grow and become emotionally balanced, even using our experience to pull others out of that place we were once in ourselves.

"Pride comes before the fall."

– P ROVERBS 16:18

CHAPTER 4

The Last Run

Four months after my mom's death, the mother of my child and I moved into our new place. I was barely home because I was spending most of my time in the hood. I'd come home, shower, play with my son, and then head back out. I was juggling multiple women at the time, trying to please them while neglecting the one who had been by my side and patient with me through it all. I never once thought to ask how she was feeling regarding my mom's death. They were really close. I was just focused on what I wanted and did not care about how my selfishness was hurting those around me.

I came into the house one morning after a long night out and was tired and hungover. We got into a huge argument over a girl that I was cheating with and it turned physical. When I grabbed my stuff to leave, she cried, yelling, "Don't go, I keep having dreams of you getting killed."

I thought that it was just one of her scare tactics to keep me home, so I replied, "Let me die then. I'm ready," and then I left.

Hen, Zaret, and Beazy were locked up during this time, which only left me and Kahlil. Kahlil noticed that I'd changed and that I was being more reckless than ever. He knew I had lost it when I almost killed a man for stealing $40 worth of crack from me. He tried his best to talk me off of the ledge that I was walking on and encouraged me to go home, but his words fell on deaf ears. He wanted to be a good friend and continue to ride with me, but even he could smell the scent of death that was lingering around me. I left him with no choice but to walk away.

I still had my cousins though, Tone and Dre, who were brothers, and Mills, who I called Baby Bro. They were part of the reason that I was stepping into a new lane of danger. They were dangerous and ruthless. And the four of us felt unstoppable. They began to call us the "A-Team." Even my hood began to turn its back on me. Mainly because I had started hanging with my cousins who were from 12th Street, and they were terrorizing everyone in every hood, including mine. We could barely go anywhere without having to shoot our way out. There were even rumors that drug lords from multiple hoods had put a hit out on us. We never had a clue from which angle it would come from, so we stayed strapped and stayed alert.

After a while, Kahlil and I began talking again. I called and apologized for telling him, "This is the street, if you're scared go to church." I missed my brother, and I needed him by my side. I felt like there was no one I could trust more than him.

One night, while doing what I once considered as having a good time, drinking and smoking with my homies, I dozed off on the couch, and I had a dream that I was at a store running and got shot in my back, then fell to the ground and died. I jumped up out of my sleep, not thinking too deeply about it, but when I dozed off again, I had the same dream. I took it as a warning the second time. We were in a vacant four-family flat home that we sold drugs out of. In the hood, we call it the "Trap." I got up and went over to the next apartment. I got down on one knee, placed my hand on the window, and prayed, "Lord, whatever you do, just don't kill me."

One day, while sitting outside, hanging with the homies, there was an outdoor church service going on in the field right next door from where we sold drugs. As I sat on the crate up against a steel black gate smoking my cigarette, I could hear the pastor preach while the people sang. He was speaking about life, how we're on borrowed time, and how we should give our life to Jesus. Then two men in suits walked up to our crew and asked to have a word with us. My homies laughed then walked away. The man looked at me and said, "God sent me here to pray for you." I felt like there was something different about this man.

I wanted to stay and talk, but before I could respond, Tone pulled up in his grey van and said, "Come on, cousin, we have a move to make." I threw my cigarette on the ground and stepped on it, stood up, and walked away toward the van. When I looked back at the man, he was staring at me, as if he knew something I didn't. I understood that the life I was living would soon have its consequences. I just thought that I would have time to straighten up before it was too late, but little did I know…my end was fast approaching.

Reflective Thought: *We look around and there are warning signs all around us, from the blinking yellow light signaling us to slow down, to the mileage meter that tells us we're going over our limit, to our parents warning us to stay away from a certain crowd of kids, and to our boss warning us not to be late again. So what causes that guy to speed past that light and get arrested? That kid who gets caught up in trouble with his peers? Or that person being fired? It's all rooted in pride. Pride blinds us and leads us to believe that we have it all figured out and are untouchable. It often takes a humbling experience to regain our sight. I always say that experience is the best teacher, but you don't have to experience everything for yourself. Instead, let others' experiences be your teacher.*

The Night I Died

It had been two weeks since that dream. Police were swarming the hood doing drug raids, so my homies and I thought it'd be smart to stash the guns and drugs and just have a small party. We invited females, brought liquor, turned the music up, and we partied. About an hour later, Kahlil got into an argument with one of the ladies over some liquor. I can't remember exactly how it started, but all I remember was Kahlil yelling at the girl and pulling out his money, saying, "I can go buy 10 of those bottles." He then tapped me, saying, "Come on Pope, let's go grab some more liquor."

It was close to midnight; our neighborhood store was closed and the only open store was the one on the Northend. I normally wouldn't go to that store at night, especially without my gun, but because the police were still out and it was the only store open, I had no choice but to go there unstrapped. I felt in the pit of my stomach that I was making a mistake by going, but Kahlil's mind was set, and I couldn't let him go by himself.

On our way, I called the mother of my child to let her know that I'd be heading home in about an hour and asked how my son was doing. I could hear him in the background babbling. I told her I love them both and that I'd see them later. Not knowing that my life had less than 15 minutes remaining.

When we arrived at the store, Kahlil and I got out. My cousin, Dre, stayed in the car with Vanessa; she was our designated driver. As Kahlil and I entered the store, I locked eyes with one of the Northend guys I went to school with as they were leaving out. I had already taken about three ecstasy pills and had a few cups of liquor on top of still grieving the loss of my mother. I felt as though I couldn't pass up an opportunity to let off some steam. As they walked past us, I leaned toward him and forcefully bumped my shoulder against his. He then turned around and threw his hands up as an act of surrender and said, "I'm Cool," and he and his guys left.

I knew it was awkward how he had just handled that situation because the guy I knew in high school would have engaged immediately. Something didn't feel right so I tapped Kahlil and said, "Let's Go!"

As soon as I stepped out of the store, there they were waiting for me. We exchanged a few words, and before I knew it, one of the guys was raising a gun and firing it at me. He shot me first in the leg. I took off running, and he continued to shoot, hitting me twice more in the leg and four times in the back. I made it two feet from Vanessa's car before my legs gave out and my body began to vibrate as if it was shutting down. I military crawled the rest of the way to the car while coughing up blood.

The guy was still shooting at me.

I managed to open her door. I remember saying to myself, "Terrence, wake up, you're only dreaming," but not this time.

My dream had come true. I couldn't believe I was out there shot and dying. I was so confused and afraid. Venessa tried her best to pull me into the car, but she struggled to pull a 300+ pound man who was now paralyzed into her vehicle. She had no choice but to let go.

Dre and Kahlil had run off and left me once the shooting started.

It was only me and God now.

Life or death.

I lay there on the ground—barely able to breathe because the bullets had punctured both my lungs—bathing in a pool of my own blood.

I could see the guy's feet coming toward me, most likely to finish me off. As he got closer, I began to make my peace with dying. I lay down and closed my eyes, preparing myself for the kill shot. But by God's grace, the police pulled in just in time. They began to exchange gunfire. The guys made it back to their van and drove off, and the police had to make a split-second decision to either go after them or stay and assist me. And thankfully, they chose me, but I was not out of the fire just yet. I still had one huge problem; I was dying.

As I lay there on the ground, fighting to stay alive, there were a million thoughts running through my mind, mostly regrets. I regretted all the poor decisions I'd made. I regretted wasting my life. I regretted not taking heed to all the warning signs. I continued thinking about my son and the fight with his mother. And now I was dying and it was too late to change any of it. My time was up. My choice was made, and now I was reaping what I'd sown and death was my reward.

I continued to fight to live, crying and begging the officers to take me to the hospital.

Dying was nothing how I had imagined it. I wasn't acting like Nino Brown. I had no last gangster remarks. I didn't even think of a cigarette. I was afraid, praying and weeping as I looked toward the clouds, praying that God would intervene.

The EMTs (Emergency Medical Technicians) were 20 minutes away, but it felt like they were taking forever. I knew if I waited any longer that I wouldn't make it, so I used what little energy and breath I had left to grab the officer's leg and said, "Please, I have a son," then I went unconscious.

When I came to, I felt him picking me up and putting me into the back of his car. I remember feeling as if I was falling into the crevice of his back seat and my body felt like it was on fire. Then it happened. My vision slowly faded, my heart slowly beating, and my fight was over.

I died.

I was rushed to the hospital, taken out of the car, put on a stretcher, and taken to the back after being shocked by a defibrillator that jumped started my heart. When I opened my eyes, I remember seeing the hospital lights fly by my eyes as I was being rushed towards the back. I remember the doctors asking me questions to keep me alert. "What's your name, a contact number, how old are you?" And I barely knew any of it.

They took me off the stretcher, placed me on an operating table, and cut my shirt open. I can still feel the cold leather table as it touched my upper back. Then I died again. I don't remember anything about the afterlife, and maybe it's for the best that I didn't, because the life I was living, I'm sure my final destination wasn't heaven.

I was gunned down on April 29, and I regained full consciousness on May 6, my mother's birthday. Talk about an angel watching over me; that was a clear sign that I could not miss.

I couldn't believe that I was still alive. I was grateful, but I started to freak out and became discouraged when I discovered I couldn't feel my legs and that there was a chance I'd never walk again. I wanted to weep like a baby. But waking up and seeing my family and some friends there staring at me with excitement, gave me a feeling that everything was going to be alright. The police came into my room the following day, asking if I knew the guys who did it, and I responded, "No." Even though I knew who did it, I knew when I joined the gang that I was under the no snitch code. I couldn't have a reputation for snitching, especially when I was the one who initiated the conflict. In addition, I wanted revenge, and I couldn't have the police getting in my way. Unfortunately, my silence only made room for that guy to hurt an innocent man later down the road. That was the first time I'd ever questioned myself regarding the snitch code. And if I had made the right decision.

An old Cherokee Indian chief was teaching his grandson about life.
"A fight is going on inside me," he told the young boy, "a fight between two wolves. The Dark one is evil—he is anger, envy, sorrow, regret, greed, arrogance, self-pity, guilt, resentment, inferiority, lies, false pride, superiority, and ego." He continued, "The Light Wolf is good—he is joy, peace, love, hope, serenity, humility, kindness, benevolence, empathy, generosity, truth, compassion, and faith. The same fight is going on inside you grandson...and inside of every other person on the face of this earth."
The grandson ponders this for a moment and then asked, "Grandfather, which wolf will win?"
The old Cherokee smiled and simply said, "The one you feed."

—UNKNOWN

CHAPTER 5

The War Within

You vs You

I spent one year in the hospital after my injury; six months recovering in ICU and another six months in a rehabilitation facility. During that time, I had a lot of time to reflect and choose what direction I wanted my life to go in from there. I felt so lost and broken. I was depressed and even contemplated suicide. I thought to myself, *I will never be the same again. Who's going to respect me now or even want to deal with a cripple? How will I defend myself?*

    I could barely hold my son on my lap or wipe my own behind. I thought to myself, *Life is over and can't anything good come from this.* For the first time in a long time, I was forced to deal with the truth and pain that I had suppressed for so long with drugs and staying busy. The death of my mother, the pain that I'd inflicted on others, the unforgiveness of my father, my feelings of abandonment, insecurity and fear, had all come rushing back like a tidal wave.

I tried pretending as if I was in severe pain, hoping that the doctors would give me some strong medication to help me escape my reality but Motrin was all that they would provide. I felt like I was drowning in the middle of the ocean and no one could save me. One afternoon, I was lying in bed, my family, girlfriend, and son had just left. I glanced over at the drawer in my rehabilitation room and spotted a blue King James Bible. It may sound crazy, but I could feel it pulling me, drawing me to pick it up. I grabbed it and began to skim through it, but I didn't understand most of the words in it. It was almost as if I was reading a mixture of English and Chinese words. I then put it back. I figured if God wanted me to read the Bible, then He would have made it easier to understand.

Later that day, there was a knock on my door. It was a pastor. He was doing his daily rounds ministering and talking to the patients. I never really allowed him into my room because I had my own perspectives of pastors at that time. I felt that they were hypocrites and liars who were filled with greed, and that their only agenda was to prey on the weak-minded and exploit them for cash. But for some reason, I felt led to give him a chance that day. I needed an encouraging word and at least he could give me that (even if it was a lie). I just needed some kind of hope.

He began to tell me what God was saying about me to him, and to my surprise, he was actually on point about a lot of things I was dealing with. But I figured he had been doing this job long enough to know what a newly injured person was going through and how many other patients he had sold this same story to that day. It was when he began to pray for me that something that had never happened started to occur.

I felt something like a surge go through my body, a peace that I'd never felt before. I began struggling to hold my tears back because I didn't want him to have the satisfaction that his con methods were working. When he was leaving, he said something that I would never forget; "God doesn't only hear my prayers, He hears yours too, and sometimes He puts us on our backs so that we can look up."

I sat thinking about that all night. I wanted to pray but I felt like I'd done too much in my life. That He didn't want to hear from me anymore. Plus, He was angry at me. Why else would He have allowed this to happen?

The pastor's prayers and words lingered through my mind for days. I wanted to change and give God a chance, to start over and just leave the streets behind me, and be there for my son, but I couldn't help but think of what people would say. "The Pope has turned into the Pope." I couldn't just give up my reputation like that, and I still had to get revenge on the guy who shot me. What would the streets think if I just let that slide?

I was fighting a war within (Me vs. Me). I was the strongest enemy that I'd ever faced, and I didn't know which side to choose.

While staying in the rehab facility, I met a lot of people who were also in wheelchairs. They were smiling, laughing, and enjoying their lives as if nothing had happened. I didn't understand how they could be so happy in their situation. I stayed away from them because I had convinced myself that my situation was only temporary and I wasn't a cripple like they were. When I was only escaping from the fact that this was now my new reality, temporarily or indefinitely. I couldn't wait to get out of that place. But honestly, I was in no rush to get back to my old life. I still had a choice to make and a wolf to feed: Was I giving up the streets or not?

Back to the Block

"If we fail to make a conscious decision about what direction our life will go in, we unconsciously end up right back where we started, or worse."

- TERRANCE J. POPE

After being released from the rehab center, I went straight home. Everything felt so different. I felt so vulnerable and helpless. I had to learn how to maneuver my wheelchair around my home, how to transfer to my bed, and even had to ask my girlfriend to pass me a cup of water. I could also tell that she looked at me differently now that I was in a wheelchair. She looked as if she wasn't sure if she could handle it, which I understood. It was new for us both, and we both needed some time to adjust to this new norm.

I would lay down in bed with my son next to me and stared at him the whole day, feeling sorry for myself. So many thoughts were going through my mind: *How will I play with him or protect him now and how will he feel when he's older, having a dad in a wheelchair?"* But I knew that if I couldn't fight for myself, at least I could fight for him.

As I sat there one day holding him, my cousin, Dre, called and said, "I'm coming in to get you, we're going out today."

Every part of me wanted to say, "I'm ok, cousin, maybe another day," because I knew our going out always ended in trouble. But I couldn't resist the chance to get out and get some fresh air after being in the hospital for a whole year. Plus, it beat lying around and feeling sorry for myself all day.

I got up and got dressed, when he arrived, I got into the car and we headed to the hood and met up with the homies. I was back where I'd started, drinking, smoking, and partying. And stirring up trouble. But this time was different than before. I couldn't help but continue to think about how I was wasting a second chance at life, how I might not be so lucky the next time, and how I was ready for something different. But fear of being seen as soft wouldn't let me tell them that. So I played along, smiling and laughing while feeling lost and sad inside. Before I knew it, I was back selling drugs and making more money than I ever had.

My doctors were writing pain medication prescriptions two to three times each month, and I was selling them on the streets for double the usual price. On top of that, I was buying crack cocaine and weed to sell and getting almost $1700 in social security. I was raking in money like it was falling off a tree. I guess the wheelchair had its perks after all. I was living life again, so I thought. Being paralyzed didn't seem like that big of an issue anymore.

I had my homies behind me everywhere I went, shielding me like I was the US president and the women were still loving me. I felt like I was on top. I was back to medicating myself with drugs to suppress the pain, the truth, and the continued calling I was feeling from God.

I bought myself a vehicle, but I had no idea how I was going to drive it. I just knew I was tired of having to wait on people. I was ready for my independence. My girlfriend at the time and I got into a huge argument. I didn't understand why she was trying to intentionally fight so much all of a sudden, but I was tired of it and ready to leave without always depending on her to take me. I got so frustrated during our argument that I broke the leg off a walker that was in our home, rolled out of the house, jumped in my car, and used the stick to drive it. I was terrified of crashing or getting caught by the police. But practice makes perfect, and I was back on the road and headed back to the block.

The Broken Cistern

I had everything I thought I wanted: money, respect, and women. I was no Big Meech, not even close, but I had a lot more than I'd ever had. And at that time, I felt as if I was on top of the world. But I couldn't help but feel like I was missing something. I was beginning to feel depressed and empty again. I could be in a room full of people and still feel alone. I tried buying things and taking more drugs, but nothing seemed to fill the void in my heart permanently.

I could still feel the pull of God that I tried so hard to ignore, and it was getting stronger. The harder I fought, it seemed like the harder He pulled. I had no clue of what was happening or why it was happening. A part of me wanted to give up the streets and pursue God but I didn't know if I was ready or if He could even use me or wanted to. I had no education, never had a job, no special skills, and could barely formulate a complete sentence without using slang or cursing. On top of all the wrong I'd done, I felt like I had nothing to offer God. I was weighed down with guilt and shame, and I couldn't even imagine God loving someone like me. I was slowly falling into a deep hole of despair, and I knew I had to do something fast.

Zaret, Hen, and Tone were all in prison. Beazy, Kahlil, and I had a falling out, and Dre and Mills were on the run for murder. They eventually got caught. Truthfully, if I had not been in this wheelchair, I would have been right beside them, facing the same charge. The A

Team was falling apart piece by piece, and I felt like God was giving me another warning to get it right.

One Sunday I felt a sudden urge to go to church. I woke my girlfriend out of her sleep and asked if she would go to church with me. We had promised my cousin who's a pastor, that when I got out of the hospital, we'd come to visit his church, and it was the perfect time to make good on that promise. At the time, I didn't know why I was going or what I was looking for because I never liked the idea of feeling like I was going to worship a white naked man hanging on a cross. Or maybe it was the thought of using God to help me get out of the wheelchair. I don't know. But I do know I felt led to go.

It was my first time back in church in a long time. When we walked in, I could immediately feel that I was exactly where I needed to be. The choir was singing and people were dancing. It reminded me of attending church with my mom as a kid and laughing at all the people who were jumping around and screaming. I must admit, it felt good to be back. I felt better than I'd felt in a long time. When the choir stopped singing, the congregation settled. The preacher stood up and began to speak.

As I sat there in the far back of the church, I couldn't help but feel like he was speaking directly to me. He was speaking on everything that I had been dealing with as if he had been a fly on the wall in my home. As he continued to speak, I felt a warm feeling in my chest. It was a feeling that I hadn't felt in a long time. It was the feeling of hope. I left there feeling whole and encouraged, and I headed right back to the hood that took no time draining me again.

I started going to church regularly, but I had not yet committed my life fully to Christ. I would go to get my feel-good dose of encouragement and head right back to the block. But the more I went, the more I began to slowly change. It started with changing how I would dress for church. I saw how the other men dressed in their nice suits, so I went and bought myself one. Then I started inquiring about a Bible. I knew I couldn't understand it, but I wanted one of my own since all the other guys carried one. Then it was going up to the altar call, getting prayed for, and saying the salvation prayer. I still had no idea what being saved meant, but it sounded good.

My older cousin, Leonard, who also attended the church and was a minister, heard that I had inquired about a Bible, and he was excited. Leonard was the first man who had ever spoken promise into my life as a child growing up. He told me that God had a plan for my life and that one day I'd be a minister for the Lord. He believed in me and had seen something in me even when nobody else did. I loved being around him, although I never told him that, because he always made me feel like I was special and loved, not only by him but by God. So when he heard I wanted a bible, he pulled me to the side after service and handed me his.

It was an NLT study Bible. It was much easier to read and even had a commentary section that broke down everything I'd read. It was a game-changer for me. I would spend hours reading it. I had no idea what was happening to me, but I liked it. But knowledge without wisdom was useless. I wasn't applying what I'd learned and leaving my old life behind. I was doing exactly what the pastor said I was doing, and that was straddling the fence. It was time for me to make a decision, to possibly live a life of permanent fulfillment or keep filling up the broken cistern. I continued to let pride, fear, a reputation, and people's opinions keep me from a life that could possibly bear fruit and fulfillment.

I know my choice should have been a no-brainer but the street life was all I'd ever known. It was what gave me a sense of worth and belonging. It accepted me when my own family wouldn't. My identity was wrapped up in it, and I didn't know who I was without it. And now I was caught between the choice to leave the known for the unknown. To trust my life to a God that I was still questioning if really existed. I at least knew what to expect from the streets. I didn't know what to expect being a Christian. I was becoming mentally exhausted from being torn between fear and faith.

Reflective Thought: *Looking in from the outside, we become in awe of street life's highlights: its glam, fame, money, power, and respect. Any kid who feels worthless, insecure, unseen, or alone may see it as an opportunity to feel some self-worth. It is one of Satan's greatest strategies; creating an illusion of hope to lead us into a hopeless pit. We never see the pain it causes, the parents that are crying, the drug addict's family who are praying, those who've gone to prison for life and are living with regret, the dead pleading from the grave for us to turn around. We don't see the kids hurting from losing their father or mother to the streets, family members feeble and weeping at funerals, how it robs of our true identity, our peace, a life of purpose, and the emptiness it brings. All we see is the glittering lie, one that overpromises and underdelivers.*

"...Old things have passed away."

CHAPTER 6

"God, I surrender"

It was around midnight as I was driving from the club, high on ecstasy and Hennessy, to pick up the mother of my child. It was pouring down with rain and thunder. I turned on the radio station, originally looking for some gangster music to ride to, when I stumbled across a gospel station.

The song "Have Your Way" by a Detroit artist named Detrick Haddon came on the radio. The song began to minister to my heart in such a way that I had to pull over, and I began to pray and cry so hard. I began to yell, "Lord, I surrender! I'm yours! I'm not running anymore! Do with me as you please! I'm tired, broken, and lost. I don't care if you're black or white, all I know is that I need you! Please reveal yourself to me." I can't remember all that I prayed that night but I sat there for almost a half-hour talking with God. Even though I can't remember every word verbatim, I do know one thing: God heard my cry.

Now, I didn't change right away, but something in me changed that night, and I was sure of it. I went back to the hood the following day, and something was different this time. I no longer desired to be there or around my friends anymore. I would try smoking and drinking and I would feel a strong conviction come over me.

When I got home, I would pray to lift the heaviness off of me. This happened to me for about a week before it became clear to me that God was doing a new thing in me and had begun setting me apart. For the first time in my life, I wasn't afraid of walking away from my old life anymore and didn't care about the opinions of people. I felt bold and empowered and confident that God had a better life awaiting me! I couldn't prove it, but somehow, I just *knew*. I was experiencing joy and hope that I had never known.

I would later learn that it was the Holy Spirit enabling me to do what I wasn't able to do on my own. It was no wonder why I had so many failed attempts to change in the past; I didn't have the life-changer (Jesus). My family and I were in a good place, and God was showing up in all kinds of ways. I sat the mother of my child down and told her that God was telling me to stop getting the pain prescriptions and selling them and that He would provide for us. She looked at me as if I had lost my mind because that was 90% of our income, and we would be giving up almost $10,000 a month. She didn't agree with my decision and tried to fight me on it, but I knew in my heart that I heard from God and that I was doing the right thing. It was even harder breaking the news to my clientele that I would no longer be supplying them and supporting their habits.

While playing the game one night, I heard God say, "Give your car to Marquita," who is my cousin and was struggling with transportation at the time.

Now I started to question if I was going crazy or if I was perhaps experiencing withdrawal side effects until the mother of my child came out of the room and said, "Terrance, why do I think God is saying give Marquita my car?"

I sat up immediately and said, "Let's call her tonight. We can give her your car since it's newer and in better condition than mine." But she refused. I called Marquita the next morning and handed her my car keys and said, "It's yours."

God was testing our obedience, and I didn't want to fail. I knew in my heart that God would bless me with something better. I was a new believer on fire and ready to give my left arm if God had asked. The more I gave up, the more God blessed me. I was seeing Him move in ways I'd never seen Him move before. From unexplained checks in my name in the mailbox to random people blessing me with gifts. If He hadn't given me anything else, what He had already given me was enough: peace of mind and joy! God was doing a new thing in me, and I was letting Him. I had given up selling and taking drugs and the streets. I was attending church regularly and on my way to being a better boyfriend and father overall. But what was to come next would test the measure of my faith in a way that I never expected, and I'd be faced with the choice of continuing to pursue God or just throwing in the towel.

Trial and Temptation

"Consider it pure joy, my brothers and sisters,[a] whenever you face trials of many kinds, 3 because you know that the testing of your faith produces perseverance. 4 Let perseverance finish its work so that you may be mature and complete, not lacking anything."

- JAMES 1:2-4

As I continued to grow in God, I began to notice a sudden change in the mother of my child. I could tell that she wanted God too, but she wasn't ready to fully commit. She enjoyed the money from the pills and the idea of having a gangster as a boyfriend, although she didn't like the idea of me being in the streets. Mainly because of the women I was messing around with. She liked having a guy from the streets who could turn a nickel into a dollar with just one flip. But I was becoming less and less of that man she met at 15 years old. She wanted me to surrender my life to her, not Christ because surrendering to God meant turning away from the sinful life we were living, and that was more than she was willing to sacrifice. That wasn't the only problem that she had with me.

I could see it in her face and actions that she didn't like the fact that I was in a wheelchair. She tried her best to tolerate it until she just couldn't anymore. She started to initiate small arguments regularly and accused me of things I had not done. One afternoon, I got so frustrated because she was constantly picking fights, and I threw a metal vase at the wall only two inches away from where she was standing. I admit I was wrong for losing my temper, and I shouldn't have thrown anything so I apologized to her. She ran into the room, grabbed her phone, and called the police.

We had gotten into worse fights than this in the past, and this time I didn't even lay a hand on her. I couldn't understand why this time was so different and made her go as far as calling the cops. I just figured she was scared. When the cops arrived, I told them what I'd done and that I was wrong. Apparently, she decided to give a different story to the other officer. She told them that I had punched her, threw this vase at her, and hit her in the head with it and that I'd threatened to kill her. I sat there feeling so confused and lost. I even began to question myself if I had really done all that she was accusing me of.

Thankfully, my god-sister was there to tell them what really happened. I could see in the officer's face that he knew she was lying. Even through all her dramatic tears and holding her head as she tried to defend her story, he could see that it was all a big act. But they still had to do their job. When they asked her if she was pressing charges, she replied, "Yes," and they had no choice but to take me in.

It was apparent that she wanted me out of the house, but instead of her just saying that, she chose to set a trap and, like a fool, I took the bait. While sitting in the precinct, I was angry. I wanted to hurt her, but I had a lot of time to think, and I figured I had done worse to her, so I could forgive her for this. The officer released me a few hours later. When I returned home, I asked her why she lied to the officer. She did not respond. For the next few days, she wouldn't speak to me, and even began to sleep in our son's room. The house felt empty, cold, and dark. I didn't even recognize her anymore.

I prayed and prayed, asking God to restore my relationship. I didn't understand why, after giving up everything and following Him, He would allow me to go through this. I called my pastor, and all he had to say was, "I'll be praying for you." I felt so lost, heartbroken, and alone.

As I sat in my room praying, crying, and begging God to speak to me, there was no answer. I sat there in the dark listening for an answer when I heard a still small voice say, "Leave." I questioned if it was God because why would He want me to leave my family. It didn't make any sense, but God was getting ready to send me on a journey that would change my life forever. A journey that would not only help me to truly discover Him but also discover who I am in Him. It didn't make sense then, but it would all make sense later.

After giving it long enough thought that night, I got up the next day to talk to her, and still no response. I asked her if it was someone else and she replied, "No." I felt that I was being punished for all that I had put her through in the past. So accepting that I was only laying in the bed that I had made for myself, I packed my clothes, kissed and hugged my son, and told her I was going to go stay at my sister's for a few days until things calmed down.

I made it to my sister, Britney's, house. She lived in a small, one-bedroom apartment with her guy friend. I slept on the couch, which was very uncomfortable for someone in a wheelchair who still had three bullets in his back that the doctors said were too chancy to remove.

I called the mother of my child to say good night to her and my son. When I hung up, I received a text from her that read, "I've found someone else, so you can stay at your sister's." I remember throwing up everything I had eaten that day. My stomach turned inside out, and I couldn't eat for weeks. All I could do was drink water. I didn't know it at the time, but I was fasting and feeding on the word of God. I was completely confused and in the dark about what was happening, but God was ordering my steps and had me right where He wanted me.

A part of me wanted to throw in the towel and just go back to the streets. I thought that when I signed up to be a Christian, that life would become easier, not harder. But I had already experienced Jesus, and He had become so real to me. My eyes were finally opened, and I could clearly see that the life I'd chosen to leave was desolate, and there was no way I could go back after knowing all that I knew now. I'd come so far and I'd seen the consequences of doing things my way. I had made my choice to follow God, and I was sticking with it. Despite what I was going through, I was determined to follow the call to a better life that I was constantly feeling.

After staying with my sister for about two weeks, I knew I had to find somewhere else to live because her apartment wasn't handicap accessible, my wheelchair was tearing up her walls, and I couldn't get in her restroom to take care of personal matters. So I had to do something that I cringed at the thought of doing, and that was call my father and ask to stay with him awhile.

By this time, he had gotten out of prison and married my stepmom, Donna, who just recently passed in October 2020. She was amazing and loved my siblings and me as if we were her own. There was nothing we could ask for that she wouldn't give us, but the biggest gift she gave us all was her unconditional love.

Moving in with my father, step-mom, stepbrothers, and sisters was bitter-sweet. I enjoyed building a relationship with them and watching them treat my son with love when he visited every weekend. My dad, on the other hand, had shown himself to be no different than he had always been. Truthfully, I was hoping that he had changed because even though he had done all that he had done in the past, I was in a place in my life where I was ready to forgive, to put that behind us and move forward. But seeing the old behavior only brought new anger and resentment. He was the same man with a different family.

In retrospect, Satan began using my father in an attempt to destroy and deter me. My father would criticize me for reading the Bible. He called me a hypocrite, saying that it wasn't possible to be a gangster one moment then a man of God the next. He would say things like, "Jesus isn't real, that's a white man's faith." He even went as far as calling me Jim Jones, a man who portrayed himself to be a man of God and is known for one of USA's biggest massacres that happened on November 18, 1978.

It was evident that he had never had an encounter with God and my life would be the only Bible he may ever read. When he noticed attacking my faith wouldn't work, he tried reminding me of my past, siding with the mother of my child in reminding me of all I'd done to her. He would say things like, "If you hadn't put her through all that you have, then you wouldn't be sleeping on my living room floor while she's in your bed with another man, who's now your son's stepdad."

He tried everything to break me. He was unaware that he was being an agent for Satan, but I was well aware of the spiritual war that was taking place before me. I continued to stand in the strength and peace of God. There were times I almost lost my patience and even wanted to give him and the mother of my child the war that they were so eagerly asking for. I struggled with submitting my pride and anger to the Lord for a while, but I understood that if I'd lost my footing, I would be giving Satan the advantage he needed to win.

By this time, I was getting $700 in social security and $300 of that was going toward my parents' rent. I was the most broke I'd been in a long time, and my father didn't hesitate to remind me of that. He even at one time suggested I start selling pills again, and honestly, it didn't sound like a bad idea, considering my circumstances. I was broke and sleeping on my father's living room floor. But I knew It was another strategy of the enemy to take my eyes off the solution and focus on the problem, causing me to forget the promise of God that He will provide.

The Restoration

> *"You intended to harm me, but God intended it for good to accomplish what is now being done, the saving of many lives."*
>
> *- GENESIS 50:20*

I stayed with my father for about six months until my younger sister, Latrice, got her place, and insisted I move in with her after witnessing my father trying every attempt to break me. I stayed with her and lived in her basement for about two years. It was a three-bedroom house, and the upstairs was occupied by her, my niece, and nephew. I honestly enjoyed being in the basement; it was my place of peace and gave me alone time with God. The only challenge I had was having to bump up and down almost 12 flights of stairs every day, but it kept my upper body in shape.

During this time, I began to discover God and myself on a deeper level. I not only became stronger spiritually but also physically. I weighed about 345 pounds. I was a big guy. I had always wanted to get in the gym and get in shape when I was able-bodied. I dreamed of being like those guys I saw on social media or on the cover of a magazine with the six-pack and huge chest. But I'd always felt that it was too much work and discipline that I did not have. But I was no longer that Terrance. I was more bold, courageous, and up for the challenge. I started using my medical transportation to take me down to the rehabilitation center where I stayed during my recovery after being shot. They had a gym in their facility, and I began to go there. It was a struggle starting off, but I stayed committed, and over time, I changed my eating habits and began working out five days a week. I was feeling more confident and physically better than I had ever felt. I lost about 80 pounds at that time, and I was loving it.

Everyone including family and friends began to notice my physical and spiritual transition. I had become an inspiration and an embodiment of change for everyone around me, but they fed me fuel to keep going. And with everyone rooting for me to win, I couldn't let them down. I even gained favor from the staff down at the rehabilitation, so much so that they asked me to be peer support for their newly injured patients, which consisted of me going room to room encouraging them. I also used it as a platform to share the gospel and how God had moved in my life over the past years. I discovered that God had given me the gift of encouragement, not only with my words but also with my actions.

What the world would consider the lowest point of my life, God was using to take me higher in Him. I had become a human slingshot that had been pulled back only to excel higher.

Although I was happy in the space that I was in, I was beginning to feel lonely and missed my boys. I hadn't met anyone yet that I felt close to like I did them. We continued to stay in touch through my transition and they accepted me for choosing to change my life for the most part. Besides them joking, calling me Pastor Pope or Pope Francis, they were ok with my lifestyle, but because it contradicted theirs, we could feel the distance that had come between us.

Struck with boredom one day, I called Beazy (Brandon), to come and get me. I wanted to get out for a while. He came by with Zaret and Kahlil. The spirit warned me when getting into the car that it was a bad idea, but I ignored it, just as I did the week before I was shot. My foolish excitement overrode my wisdom.

As I rode in the passenger seat, the hip-hop music that I'd fasted from for so long played. While they smoked their weed and cigarettes, I'd already started to regret going. My spirit became disturbed and wisdom screamed, "Terrance, go back home!" Yet, I was being passive, and not telling them to take me back home. I didn't want him to feel like he just wasted his gas or that I was too good to hang with them, I just smiled and continued to ride. But my passiveness would almost cause me to lose my life once again.

They decided to stop at a store, not just any store, but the same store where I was shot. And not only was it the same store, but they parked in the exact same spot where I died. They got out to go into the store and not even one minute inside, the van we came in was being shot at. By the grace of God, I wasn't hit. But it was clear that God was speaking and I wasn't about to make Him repeat Himself.

I went home after and began to pray and tell God that I was sorry for ignoring the spirit, how I felt alone in this walk and that I needed some godly friends. It was obvious that I still had a lot of growing to do, and without any accountability, I was certain to repeat the same mistakes.

Reflective Thought: *Your life should consist of three groups of people: a mentor, a mentee, and a select group of people that represent where you are in your journey. All three of you hold each other accountable in your own way. Without accountability, there's no stability in our journey. We tend to fall to the left or right, like trying to walk a tightrope for the first time and never arriving on the other side. Because my brothers had no biblical foundation, they weren't able to hold me up as I walked the type rope of* *righteousness. Instead, I was pulled in a different direction, almost causing me to lose focus of the assignment. A mentor's job is to pull you up; your job is to pull your mentee up. And those who walk beside you, you all have the responsibility to hold each other up as you all move forward in your journey.*

"In the pursuit to change lives, my life was changed. In the pursuit to heal others, I discovered healing for myself."

— Terrance J Pope.

CHAPTER 7

Authentic Manhood

Lisa Johanna is a pastor who has known me since I was six years old. She was the first to introduce me to Christ as a kid through her Christian youth program my siblings and I attended every Friday night. She had heard I'd committed my life to Christ and called me one evening, asking if I wanted to come to a men's group called the "B.O.M.B SQUAD," an acronym for bring our men back . I declined because it was in the neighborhood I once ran in, and I had no desire to be back in that area. But Lisa has a way of getting what she wants. She's like the Caucasian mom I never had. She'll only ask nicely once. So when she said, "Ok, I'll be picking you up at 5:00 pm," I knew to be dressed and ready to head out when she arrived.

Once we arrived at the facility, I saw a few guys I grew up with and some I still considered friends, standing with a group of distinguished older men I'd never seen before. These men were different; they weren't like the church-going men that I was used to. The suit-wearing, Bible carrying, preaching all the time, and so serious. They were just regular men who expressed their love for God and their joy in helping men to discover authentic manhood.

They laughed, cracked jokes with us, were transparent about their shortcomings, didn't try to make us feel below them, and met us where we were and adjusted accordingly. I didn't even know who the pastor was until after the program. He never even introduced himself as a pastor, but simply called himself Stacey. He eradicated every tainted thought I had about pastors. He was wise, transparent, and showed vulnerability. He laughed and loved me as if he knew me forever, and so did the guys he was with. And I was inspired by them and felt like I'd known them forever as well. I was sold and knew that these were the men God had placed in my life that I prayed for only a week prior.

I began going to Pastor Stacey's church and joined after two weeks. He's a theologian, and it was evident. He was the first pastor to educate me on the grace of God and broke down what salvation meant for me and the essential roles of the trinity (God, Jesus, Holy Spirit). I began to mature spirituality and became biblically educated under his leadership

B.O.M.B Squad in my neighborhood was a try-out in our area, but it didn't go so well because most of the guys in my neighborhood weren't taking it seriously. The real B.O.M.B Squad took place at the church I would eventually join. It started at 6:00 am in the morning.

Pastor Stacey set it at that time because he wanted men to make the sacrifice and get used to getting up at 6:00 am to meet with God.

My first time there would change my life and perspective forever. When I rolled in, there were over 100 men in the room, all different races and professions. They were talking, laughing, hugging, and encouraging one another. I had never witnessed anything like this in my life. Where I'm from, this many men in one room was bound to end in a fight or shoot out. This was foreign to me.

I scanned the room, looking for the guys I had met in my neighborhood B.O.M.B Squad meeting. I spotted one of the guys I had met and went and sat next to him. Only a few minutes in, guys were coming over to introduce themselves, and hugging me. I felt so uncomfortable because I couldn't remember the last time I hugged a guy, if ever, and in my hood, that was considered a red flag and you'd seem pretty suspect.

It was clear that although I was carrying my cross, I was also still carrying a world's perspective, and God knew that part of me needed addressing and development. These men weren't operating from a world's perspective but from a heavenly one instead. They were secure in themselves. Pride, ego, competitiveness, jealousy, and envy weren't a struggle amongst them like where I'd come from. They uplifted, affirmed, cried, and bore each other's burdens.

They encouraged marriage, faithfulness, righteousness, unity, transparency, and change. All the things that are contrary to the hood.

And they all desired to know God on an intimate level and grow spiritually. They weren't perfect, and they weren't pretending to be, but they were pursuing a perfect God, and that's all that mattered. They were completely eradicating everything I grew up believing a real man was.

This group even changed my perspective on cops when I became good friends with two of them In the group. I felt like I was a part of something BIG, and not like how I did when I first got in a gang, because then I was going in to hurt the world, whereas this time I was going in to heal it. Back then I was a boy, and now I was a man.

After attending B.O.M.B Squad for a while, I met Cameron, who became my big brother and mentor. We had a funny start. He's a tall, light-skinned guy, and he was super cool. After talking one day and getting ready to leave the B.O.M.B Squad, he hugged me and said, "I love you." I can't lie, I cringed so hard and then thought to myself, *This guy is gay.* We laugh at that up until this day. After a while, I discovered that's just who he is and not only him. The majority of the guys there were affectionate men, and they didn't mind expressing their love for a brother. Their culture, (the kingdom culture) slowly rubbed off on me. The stern, unfriendly face I went with slowly became welcoming and was accompanied by a smile.

At this time, I moved out of my sister's house and into a low-income apartment, still in shock that how what should have been a two-three-year waiting list had only taken two weeks. On top of that, a DTE bill of over $3,000 that almost prevented me from being able to move in miraculously cleared a week before my move-in date. God had begun to restore everything that I had lost as He promised.

I was blessed with a van by a lady I'd only met a handful of times. Before she passed, she put my name in her will for her van. The van was very old and rusty and needed a lot of work. I was grateful, but I couldn't help but ask God, "Is this the vehicle you promised me?" At that time, I didn't have my license either. I knew that God is a God of order, so why would He give me a van with no license? It didn't make any sense. But with the excitement to begin driving it, I started out on a journey to get my license.

I owed over $5000 in tickets and had four warrants in four different counties. I had no idea of how I was going to clear all this up without having to spend time in jail. I was only getting $700 in social security and that was going into rent, utilities, and groceries. All I had was God and faith, and that was all I needed. I stepped out in BOLDNESS and began to go to court for my tickets, and that's when God started to move. A few of my cases were dismissed and warrants were lifted. I was putting my faith in work into action. But I was still left with a little over $3500 to pay before being able to get my license.

Cameron knew that I was trying to get my license, but he never asked if I'd needed any help, and I never asked him for any because him pouring into my life was already enough. But little to my knowledge, he was working behind the scenes. He had assembled all the B.O.M.B Squad brothers to pitch in with helping me get my license.

On our B.O.M.B squad graduation day, after the last guy received his sword of integrity, Cameron called me up to the front along with my son and began to share my heartfelt story with the congregation. When he was done, Pastor Stacey handed me a white envelope with just over $3500; the exact amount I needed. It was evident this was a move of God once again. Talk about bearing each other's burdens. These guys were exemplifying true brotherhood, and they were not only going to church but they were being the church.

After getting my license, I was blessed with a 2007 white, clean Saturn Vue through a rehabilitation program I was in. It all made sense. God never intended for me to drive the van I was blessed with the first time, but it was used as an incentive to get me moving to obtain my license, so I could receive the blessing He had for me. It reminded me of the saying, "You're not waiting on God, God is waiting on you." I had brotherhood and a clear perspective on manhood. I was discovering more of myself and God. But most importantly, I felt free, free to be the very person I'd neglected for so many years: ME.

"In order to experience true external freedom, we must first remove the internal barriers."

–Terrance J Pope

CHAPTER 8

"A Step Back to Move Forward"

Through the same rehabilitation program that supplied me with my Saturn Vue, I was given my first job. My counselor loved the impact I was making on the patients as a peer supporter so much that he suggested that I stop doing voluntary work and fill out an application at the mental health facility that he was currently working in. I did, and I was soon hired! I was so excited to be working and doing what I love: changing lives. I felt like I was going to be the Superman of my job, rescuing people from their brokenness and sadness, and restoring them back to their whole state. I was getting ready to bring God's kingdom on earth.

I worked as a peer support specialist. And as I sat and talked with the patients who we called members, something began to happen. I got the chance to hear the hearts and stories of a murderer, homosexuals, people who were addicted to drugs, pedophiles, those who suffered from depression, schizophrenia, etc. It began to humble me in a way that I never imagined. Hearing a guy confess to me that he was sexually attracted to his daughter, caused me to discipline my anger; talking to a homosexual and learning how he was raped by his stepfather for years helped me to better understand him and his choice; and finally, talking to a mother waiting in a lobby for her daughter, who I once sold drugs, to get out of a substance abuse program, made me realize how I was not only destroying one person by selling drugs in my past, but I was hurting a whole family.

What also impacted me in a way that I least expected was talking to those who suffered from mental health. I started to see a bit of myself in each of them. Some of the things they were experiencing I had or was experiencing myself. Like mood swings, being afraid to trust and love fully because of the thought of losing someone, or being betrayed. The repeated thoughts of doubt and fear and self-sabotaging conversation with myself. I was experiencing sadness, frustration, happiness, and tiredness, all in one day. I started reading up on mental health diagnoses and discovered I had my own mental health problems that needed to be addressed. It became evident that God not only brought me here to help change lives but also to change mine. It was time I dug up and put to rest the things that I had buried alive that were haunting me from the grave.

In the Black community, most interpret having a therapist as admitting that you're "crazy," so we tend to reject seeking the help that we need. Sometimes out of pride, and other times because dealing with up and down emotions and behaviors for so long becomes a norm, causing the conclusion to be drawn that that's just who we are and how we're made, failing to realize that life's challenges have infiltrated our hearts and minds, causing a malfunction. I wrestled with the thought of getting a therapist because of pride, but I knew that it was time to go inward so that I could excel outward. I signed up as a patient (member) where I worked.

Going through therapy was a game-changer for me. It challenged me to go back and deal with unresolved issues. Like the passing of my mother, the anger towards my dad, and those who had mistreated me as a kid. I discovered where my insecurities, doubts, and fears had stemmed from, the need to fit in and why I was so afraid to love, trust, and more.

A lot of people don't know that I was diagnosed with depression. They see my smile, laughter, perseverance, and ethics in my wheelchair and assume that I have it all together. But the truth is, I don't. I still have self-sabotaging thoughts trying to creep in and deter me from a life of purpose and joy. I still attend therapy to this day. I actually love going and having someone to talk to that understands my situation. It's an essential piece that helps me maintain a well-rounded life. What I've learned is that being a man is not just about taking care of bills, your hygiene, family, friends, etc., but it's also taking care of your mental health. You may have heard the saying,

"Cut the head off the chicken and the body will fall." This means that if you want to stop a group of people, you have to destroy the leader. Your mind is leading your body, and if you fail to take care of your mind, not only will you suffer but those who depend on you will too.

Mind Jogger: *"Seeking therapy or counseling doesn't mean that you're crazy, it simply means that we're HUMAN. Every day we are experiencing LIFE and are constantly gathering information about our experiences and our encounters with people, storing this information daily, somewhere within US! It's usually not until something happens that we get to see the reality of those things we've stored up, be it [good or bad]. The job of a counselor (or therapist) is not to judge you, but to simply assist in navigating through, sometimes, years' worth of [internal] files to place proper definition, expose lie-based beliefs systems about ourselves and subsequently, others where they hinder us and replace them with truth [that frees us] to the quality life and relationships that we are purposed and predestined to have; both in our homes and in our everyday lives."*

- AYANNA POPE, COUNSELOR

"If you believe God for a new car, you must get the old one out of the driveway."

– STEVE HARVEY

CHAPTER 9

He Who Finds a Wife

Waiting on the Lord

After God had given me almost everything that was taken or I was led to let go of, such as my peace, confidence, a home, a car, etc., there was still one thing I was still believing Him for: a wife.

I was still struggling with fornication; I had not practiced celibacy yet. I wanted to, but the thought of going without sex just gave me anxiety. I still believed that part of me is what made me a man, and giving it up until I was married, whenever that would have been, was a challenge. I would have been betting on a possibility. I knew that God was able to give me a wife, I just didn't know when and the thought of waiting for a long time robbed me of my patience and my discipline to wait on the Lord. I was limiting God's ability because of my hastiness which I believe delayed my blessing.

I'd finally build up the courage to be celibate after dealing with conviction after conviction. It was the last time I was intimate with a woman that I believe moved the heart of God. One afternoon after being intimate, I laid my head against the wall and cried and prayed to ask God to forgive me for my constant, conscious decision to sin against Him. I knew I wanted a wife, but I also knew that the way God and I relationship was, I would have to sacrifice my sinful desire to receive the promise. I repented and made a covenant with God to be celibate until I was married. I still casually dated in search of finding that right one, but no one had fit the ideal wife I had in mind. I had a vivid picture of the wife I wanted in mind from the way she looked to how she would act and even how we would meet. But the truth is God doesn't always give us what we want but what we need.

One early Sunday service, a woman who I'd never seen came to lead our praise and worship team. She didn't look like the woman I had imagined for so long, but she was beautiful and had the voice of an angel. There was something about her that was different. I had not even courted her and already felt like I knew her.

Time had passed after the first time I saw her when she had come back to my then church to sing at an event that we had every year. I performed a couple of my Christian rap songs that day and she went on after me, performing her songs. I sat glazing at her as she sang, feeling as though I had to get to know her. After she was done singing, she stood in the church lobby, selling her books. Not only was she a talented singer, but she also took her purpose seriously, and most importantly, she loved the Lord.

As I headed over to her book stand, I can still remember her beautiful smile as she greeted me saying, "Hello." I was super nervous, but I knew I had to make my move before she left again. I introduced myself, and we talked briefly about our performance and her books. When I left, I continued to think about her so much that I searched for her on social media, and when I found her page, I sent her a friend request. We began chatting and, immediately, I knew she was the one God intended for me.

Becoming One

After dating for a while, I began to want further confirmation from God that she was the one. I mean, she was everything I needed, but I didn't want to go before God's timetable and make a decision prematurely. So I spent a lot of time praying and asking God for signs, and He would always confirm that she was the one. One time, I even asked if He would allow a plane to pass by my apartment window if she was the one He wanted me to marry, and believe it or not, one did. What I loved about her most was that she accepted me for who I was. She didn't see an ex-gang member in a wheel chair. She saw the man I was becoming and potential that I hadn't yet seen in myself. We dated

11 months before I asked her to marry me, and we got married nine months after.

Some say the first year of marriage is rough. I don't think that's a generalized statement, but for us, it was true. Before we were married, we had unhealthy disagreements that we sought out counseling for from our pastors at that time, but because our church was transitioning in leadership and buildings, we were unconsciously looked over. My former pastor once told me, "Marriage is not to make you happy but holy," and I was about to be exposed to a side of me that I thought was dead, but it's not until we're put back into a circumstance that we realize just how that person is still alive.

I hadn't yet developed my communication skills when it came to conflict resolution. When I felt unheard, that nine-year-old kid stood up in me to scream for attention and it flowed out as aggression. And when I didn't know how to articulate my emotions, it flowed out as hurtful words. My insecurities had started flowing back in as if the dam keeping me shielded had broken.

I didn't know how to handle a woman that was confident in who she was, dedicated to her purpose, and whose trust was in God. To be honest, I was intimidated, and I found myself bringing old methods into a new operation to gain my respect, which was ineffective. She wasn't my child's mother or any woman that I'd been with in my past who submitted to my foolishness. After repeated fights and her threatening to leave, I knew I had to get my act together because if I wasn't certain about anything in my life, I was certain that I didn't want to lose her. She was the embodiment of Proverbs 31 woman. She wasn't perfect, but she was perfect for me, and I was willing to do what was necessary to keep her.

I realized that I was once again identifying with my biological dad and not my spiritual Father. I felt trapped in my thoughts, not knowing how I would change or what it'd take. It was obvious I had some deep-rooted issues and needed a spiritual intervention. I had honestly thought when I got married that I had finally arrived, but it was only another door to a detour that I had to take to become one with my wife. So I started getting one on one therapy sessions and we started marriage counseling, which should have been done long before we said our I do's. I started one on one sessions with my pastor, learning how to be a king to his queen and even calling my other married brothers to get extra information on how to lead as a husband, and I began to grow, not only as a husband but also as a leader and father.

We may have started off rough, but it was in my power to either continue the rocky road or to level the ground and I chose to reconstruct.

Helpmate

"The Lord, after creating Adam, saw that he was alone in the garden, and declared, "It is not good that the man should be alone; I will make him a help meet for him.""

- GENESIS. 2:18.

Some men read Genesis 2:18 and misinterpret it. Believing that they could assign their woman to any task and demanding them to accomplish it. They are clearly mistaking the context of this scripture. Here, God is creating Eve to be a partner to Adam, not a doormat. To help fulfill the assignment God allocated to Adam. A helpmate doesn't end there; she also helps with making wise and rational decisions, challenging you in your most complacent areas, praying for you, encouraging you, and calling you up. I can go on and on about the characters of a helpmate, but first, let me tell you about mine.

I want to start off by saying that had it not been for my wife, I wouldn't be half the man, father, and leader I am today. She has made me better in ways I couldn't imagine. She is one of the reasons I have full custody of my son, press through difficulties, believe in myself, and even the reason why I finished this book. She encouraged me to not set limits but to set the bar. To press through when the pressure is on and to stand out when everyone else is conforming. She is my wife, my manager, my coach, and my inspiration. She is God's undeserved grace.

When my wife came into my life, I struggled with time management and discipline when it came to executing my goals. I also struggled with seeing myself as a leader or believing I could ever be one. But she encouraged me and affirmed me in my weakest areas.

My wife is not only my partner in a divine union but also my partner in purpose, challenges, victories, decision making, and parenting.

That is what a helpmate is for, not to control, dominate, and dehumanize. Those are the characteristics of a boy, not an authentic man.

Seeing Her Through God's Eyes

When a man seeks to find a wife, he must first know the purpose of marriage, and that revelation comes from the one who proposed it: God.

When I got married, I had what I like to call a utopian perspective. There would be no strife, we'd be in love, googly-eyed, praying in and reading the word 24-7. Boy was I in for a reality check. As I stated in the previous chapter, we would find ourselves ready to file for divorce, not even a year in. There were things I didn't like about her and vice-versa. It's easy to keep up appearances at the beginning of the dating stage. It's not until you become one that you are exposed to the good, the bad, and the ugly, and that's when the vows, "For better or for worse," become practical.

During our counsel sessions, I learned not to see my wife in the physical but the spiritual. The statement, "I'm only human," took on a brand-new meaning for me. In the beginning, I was quick to criticize her instead of extending the same grace God had shown me. Isn't it funny how we're quick to count someone out after offending us? But we expect God to forgive us every time we offend Him. I've trained my eyes to see the best in her and count five good things for every wrong one. We already live in a world where the media capitalize on the negative, why bring it into your home?

> "Therefore, if any man be in Christ, he is a new creature: old things are passed away; behold, all things have become new."
>
> – 2 Corinthians 5:17

CHAPTER 10

True Identity

When giving up the streets and accepting Christ, I had no idea of the blessings I would receive, the joy I would experience, and the community I would have. I have become a new man, not perfect, but perfectly transformed in Christ. Unlike when I was in the streets, broken, confused, and struggling with an identity crisis. I'm finally healed and healing, have clarity, and know who I am. Who I was in my past doesn't even matter anymore. The respect, the fear I instilled in others, the money I made, and the accolades I received, I count it all as a loss.

My only concern is what's ahead. Like Paul says in Philippians 3:7-16, "But whatever gain I had, I counted as loss for the sake of Christ. Indeed, I count everything as loss because of the surpassing worth of knowing Christ Jesus my Lord. For his sake, I have suffered the loss of all things and count them as rubbish, in order that I may gain Christ and be found in him."

I am now pressing toward the mark: Philippians 3:14. Now, I don't want to give you the impression that when accepting Christ that you are exempt from troubles. No, it's quite the opposite. I've learned that when giving our life to Christ, we have been recruited into a spiritual army and the good news is we're fighting from a place of victory, not for victory. Many Christians give up because they haven't fully grasped that concept. Hoping in God never ends in shame: Romans 5:5. He'll never let us down. They abort the missions because they fail to understand the assignment, and that's standing on God's word.

Had I aborted the mission, I wouldn't have met my wife, would never have gotten custody of my son, met great friends, and mentors. I wouldn't be where I am today. I'd probably be dead, in prison, or somewhere strung out on drugs like most of the guys I grew up with. But because I know who I am and whose I am, I continue to fight, putting on the full armor of God, to prepare for the battle ahead. One of Satan's greatest mistakes was allowing me to discover my true identity in Christ because it broke the chains of confusion and opened my eyes to clarity. It shattered the shackles of conformity around my ankle, and I went running toward freedom.

CONCLUSION

My journey to manhood wasn't an easy one, but it was well worth it. The challenges, the fight, the tears, the losses, and the heartbreaks that I endured made me the man I am today. Although I faced many challenges, the greatest one that I faced was reconditioning my mind, choosing to be different in a world of conformity.

Each day, I choose to be better, to being a better father to my son than my father was to me. As a man, and because of my struggles, I now know the importance of loving a child, affirming that child, and modeling authentic manhood before him.

In 2020, I gained full custody of my son after his mother tried every means to keep him away from me because of jealousy and bitterness. Once I got married to my beautiful wife and had been exalted by God, it created strife between us. Since gaining custody of my son, I have become a better man and because of that, my son now has a better chance than the one that I was given. Contrary to the relationship between my dad and I, my son and I love, laugh, and live every day learning each other. I teach him about decision making, to be respectful, to love and to be a better man than I was. It is through my experiences that I can teach him these things. So, if you ask me whether I regret my past, I would give you a firm no in response. Everything that I have been through, all the pain that I experienced even in my childhood, have made me who I am today. They have equipped me to equip him.

As for my wife and I, we are still learning and loving each other more and more each day. We are in that space of discovering how God wants to use us as a unit to be impactful for his kingdom agenda. Little by little the pieces are coming together to form a picture that we would have never thought to pray for. Currently, we are trying to conceive our first child together. I'm believing God for this miracle.

As for the A Team, Dre is still doing life in prison. Kahlil has settled down and is now a family man. Beazy is currently locked up and I am happy to say that he has recently given his life to Christ. Zaret is on the run from the police for a gun charge, while Mills is still in the streets. Hen is now a working man and Tone just came home from prison. You may be wondering what my relationship is like with them now. Well, it's not what it once was because I have chosen a different lifestyle and we have grown up. It has become a source of great distance between us all but the love is still mutual. For the rest of them who have not yet given their lives to Christ, I am still praying that one day they will. I call to check on most of them periodically. I've become the friend that they vent to and ask for prayer when needed. I am still "The Pope" to them (look at the irony in that). I will always love my brothers and will always be here for them. Maybe not in the way that I once was in the streets, I don't go to war for them physically anymore but spiritually, I still do and always will.

My hope is that this book has inspired you. I hope that it helps you to believe that the power of God is real and change is possible. You were uniquely designed by God for a special purpose, and Jesus died so that purpose could be fulfilled in you. Jeremiah 29:11 says, "For I know the plans I have for you,' declares the Lord, 'plans to prosper you and not to harm you, plans to give you a hope and a future."

Submit to Christ and allow Him to guide you, for the reward is great. An unimaginable life and journey awaits you.

> We often say experience is the best teacher, and I agree, but we don't have to experience it but simply learn through others' experiences.
>
> – Terrance J. Pope

LIFE LESSONS

Everyone can't Go!

Someone once told me a long time ago that "Where God is taking you, everyone won't be able to go. When choosing to change the people around you will either step up or step down, regardless, you must continue forward."

After giving my life to Christ, I started noticing friends and family members becoming distant. I felt alone and like an outcast. Phone calls and visits became less and less. Honestly, I started to regret changing my life. I missed the laughs and the conversations. I was even tempted to compromise to show that I could still be fun. But the spirit within wouldn't allow me to be comfortable in sin.

It was clear that God had set me apart, not only did I feel it, but my peers did too, even if they couldn't identify what it was. I was being stretched and taken into the wilderness to spiritually grow, and it was vital that I did it alone. In retrospect, I've learned that it was nothing I'd done to make them leave, but what God was doing to develop me.

When changing our lives, we go through three seasons: revelation— when our eyes are open to truth, isolation—the period of being alone for insight and development, and elevation—the period where you are ready to excel. Be prepared for your desolation season. You may interpret people leaving as if you did something wrong, but it's the opposite. God is clearing the way to reward you for doing something right. The waiting season may be lonely and uncomfortable, but the harvest season will bear much fruit.

Is there someone or a group of people that you feel God is distancing you from? Think about your convictions. The things that you know that you ought to be doing. The areas of your life, character, and habits that you know that you could afford to do better! Who are those people who are in opposition to your change? Who, instead of embracing a new and improving you, is determined to make it an uphill battle for you by tempting, bad-mouthing, mocking, or even ostracizing you when you could really use their support? These are the people that you might want to consider setting boundaries with. Healthy boundaries allow us to still be effective in the lives of those who might need what we have to offer (help) while limiting the access that they have to us dumping what might kill, slow down, or deter us.

Who are those people who are slowing you down, killing your ambition, and deterring you from your goals of doing and being better?

How can you create healthy boundaries that say, "I'm worth more than this. I'm better than this?"

Write below:

What are some ways that you can begin surrounding yourself with people who are more like-minded, that will challenge you further into becoming all that you were purposed to be?

Use the lines below to write down your answers to these questions that will help you to gain clarity and to make a greater commitment to yourself to stay on the course of <u>change</u>!

_____
_____
_____
_____
_____
_____
_____
_____
_____
_____
_____
_____
_____
_____

Scripture: John 15:18-19, "If the world hates you, you know that it hated Me before it hated you. If you were of the world, the world would love its own. Yet because you are not of the world, but I chose you out of the world, therefore the world hates you."

Change

When it comes to change, there are three key elements that we must accept before transforming into the person we hope to be:

- Accepting where you are
- Accepting you need help
- Accepting the challenge

In arriving at your desired destination, you first have to accept your starting point. Take your GPS, for example. It starts at your current location before navigating you to your desired one. It never starts in the past or the future, but the present, and that's where you must start. Being honest with where you are is your starting point and helps you get a sense of direction. When I chose to change my life, I had to first accept that I was lost, broken, and weary. Accepting those truths became my catalyst to a road of healing and revival.

Accepting Help

Now, I know this one can be challenging, especially with the time we're living in. Everyone prides themselves on being independent and people are afraid to trust. But trust me when I say this, no one had ever made it to the pinnacle alone. We all need help when seeking people to help us grow. It's just discerning who to ask.

For me, I sought out men who were where I desired to be and who had the same qualities and values I wanted. Surround yourself with evolving people and typically what happens is someone will begin to assist you on your journey. If you feel like no one notices you, don't be afraid to grab the attention of someone you admire and ask him/her for help. Above all else, pray and ask God to bring people into your life to assist you on your journey toward transformation.

Accepting the Challenge

This step comes after accepting where you are and accepting help.

God-assigned people will begin to see your hunger for change and start purposely pushing you toward your destination. You'll know these people by the way they encourage you, affirm you, and pour into your life with words or monetary gifts, challenging you to be all who God called you to be. Just as my God-assigned people did. You must not resist but walk boldly, accepting that it won't be easy but well worth it. Trust the process, but most importantly, trust God.

People always say, "Terrance, I can't believe the rough life you had. It must be hard."

Granted I had a pretty rough life, but the hardest part of my life was choosing to change. Stripping myself of all bad habits, thought patterns, my environment, the company I kept, and reconditioning my mind and behavior.

What I'm saying is change isn't easy, and it's not for the weak. But for the one who feels it deep in your core, you were created for more, and if you are reading this, then I'm 100% certain that is you. I know that the odds may be against you and everything around you screams failure, but take it from someone who defied the odds. Following these three elements, you can, and you will SUCCEED.

What are some things that you want to change?

Write below:

1. What is it that you want to change?
2. What is holding you back from changing it?
3. How would that change affect your future? Your children's future?
4. Are you ready to make that change now?

_____
_____
_____
_____
_____
_____
_____
_____
_____
_____
_____
_____
_____
_____

Scripture: Isaiah 43:19, "See, I am doing a new thing! Now it springs up; do you not perceive it? I am making a way in the wilderness and streams in the wasteland."

Weight of Life

By the time you read this book, I am hoping to be a USA Para Powerlifter. Working out has taught me so many valuable life lessons, for example, when weight lifting, we must progressively add on pounds and do more reps to get stronger and build endurance. Such is the weight of life, resistance causes us to grow, and pressing through builds perseverance. Had it not been for the troubles I had faced, I wouldn't be who I am today. We often see trials as a means to destroy us, but I've learned to see it as something that comes to build our character, strengthen our faith, and increase our endurance.

I also fell in love with doing resistance band workouts. At first, I thought it was pointless and ineffective. I mean, I'm a 300+ bencher, why would I use a resistance band? Little did I know, bands can be more efficient than heavy weight lifting when used properly. Weight lifting focuses mostly on building the bigger muscles while bands focus on building the smaller muscles, which build your foundation (your tendons) to prevent injury. You can research it a little more if you like.

Just like resistance bands, you have to begin building your foundation, affirming yourself, reading the Word, praying, and meditating on good things, so when the weight of life comes, you'll have firm footing and not be easily broken.

When I got into powerlifting, I made the mistake of continuing to train like a bodybuilder in a Powerlifting arena, which didn't end well. I ended up injuring my shoulder and had to start all over. I went from lifting 300 pounds to only lifting 70 pounds within a week. I learned two important lessons throughout that process:

1. Humility - understanding I didn't know it all and being willing to submit myself under the authority of someone else.
2. Patience - learning to trust the process and God because He is where true strength comes from.

I also got a spiritual revelation. Trying to step into Powerlifting with bodybuilding tactics is like trying to fight a spiritual war with worldly strategies, it'll always end in failure.

Challenges expose our foundation. They let us know if we have built our life on concrete or quicksand.

When you are faced with challenges, how do you respond? Do you respond with faith, trusting God to fight your battle and going forward, OR do you respond with fear, backing down from the challenge and retreating?

Write below:

1. What challenges are you facing?
2. What steps will you take to overcome these challenges?
3. Will you believe God's word or what's in front of you?
4. How will you feel once you've overcome these challenges?
5. Are you ready to face your challenges now?

_____

_____

_____

_____

_____

_____

_____

_____

_____

_____

_____

_____

_____

_____

Scripture: James 1:2-4: "Consider it pure joy, my brothers and sisters, whenever you face trials of many kinds, because you know that the testing of your faith produces perseverance. Let perseverance finish its work so that you may be mature and complete, not lacking anything."

Eagle Eye

As I stated before, our trials are the catalysts to our growth. One of many benefits to life's challenges is the enhancement of our ability to see. When we feel we are at the pinnacle of life we often move so fast that we ignore the blessings that surround us. We rarely take the time to stop and smell the roses, stare at the vast blue sky, and pray to our lord.

Before getting shot, my life was like a train going at full speed. I was selfish and greedy. All that mattered was my desires. It cost me time with my mother, my son, my legs, peace, and almost my life. After getting injured, my perspective shifted; I saw life through a different pair of shades. I was an eagle soaring over the horizon, gazing at the beautiful and ugly areas I'd overlooked. I confronted my insecurities and accepted my uniqueness. I'm able to see life as a beautiful journey and not an ugly road. I've learned to love and value those close to me through words and action. I've learned patience, discipline, my strengths, compassion, and sacrificing time for those in need.

When facing many trials, train your eyes to see the unique shapes in broken glass or the resting period for a bird with a broken wing. Life is full of beauty, sometimes it takes hardships to see its glory.

Write below:

1. What challenges have you faced that have helped you to grow emotionally and spiritually?
2. What have you learned from those challenges?
3. How will you view the next challenge you face?

_____
_____
_____
_____
_____
_____
_____
_____
_____
_____
_____
_____
_____
_____
_____
_____

Scripture: Psalms 19:18: "Open my eyes to see the wonderful truths in your instructions."

Lift Every Voice

I discovered my talent for public speaking through a friend of mine. She invited me to her church to share my testimony at their Christmas service. Boy was I nervous! When I arrived, there were over 2,000 people waiting to hear what I had to say. So many thoughts went through my head like, *I'm not articulate enough, no one wants to hear what I have to say. I'm just a no-good guy from the streets,* and something we have all said to ourselves, *Why me?*

When it was finally time for me to speak, I rolled on stage, palms sweaty and hands shaking. Fear had engulfed me, but I took a deep breath and quoted Joshua 1:9. My friend, Lisa, handed me the mic. I lifted my voice and began to share my story. When I was done, the crowd was in tears. After it was over, so many people came to me in the hallway saying how I had changed their lives forever. But what impacted me the most was when a little kid came to me and said, "Sir, you are my hero. Can I have your autograph?"

That day made me realize how important and impactful it is to share your experience. Your words have the ability to move mountains in your life and in the lives of others. So next time you are given the opportunity to tell your story, lift your voice and share. Be someone's hero.

"When you find the courage to use your voice, it has the power to positively inspire and change the lives of others. It's one of the special gifts you have to offer the world and it's something to be cherished and championed never hidden."

- NICOLE O'NEILL

Write below:

1. How can you use your voice to help someone else?
2. Have you shared your story to encourage someone?
3. If so, how did it make you feel?

_____
_____
_____
_____
_____
_____
_____
_____
_____
_____
_____
_____

Scripture: 1 Peter 4:10-11: "God has given each of you a gift from his great variety of spiritual gifts. Use them well to serve one another."

Forgiveness

"To forgive is to set a prisoner free and discover that the prisoner is you."

- LEWIS B. SMEDES

I held a grudge against my dad for as long as I could remember. What he did to our family impacted us long after he had gone to prison. I was angry with how he treated my mother and me, and I was even angrier that I was imitating him. When he came home from prison, I tried letting go of all he had done, but seeing that he hadn't changed much made it hard. I became standoffish and resentful. I was making him pay for his actions, but what it cost me was way more. It robbed me of my peace.

Thinking so much about how he'd mistreated us as kids was blinding me from considering what he had gone through as a child and how it was affecting his thoughts and behaviors. I finally got a chance to hear his story and understood him better. And although he has a long way to go, I can appreciate where he is now.

I forgive him, but it doesn't mean that what he did still doesn't hurt, or even that I have to hang out with him often. What it means is that I'm no longer allowing him to take up space in my mind and heart and keep me prisoner to anger. I chose to let go. Hey, maybe one day he'll do a complete 180. I won't wait on it, but I'll be there with open arms, ready to embrace him if he does. I've learned through this journey to be quick to listen and slow to speak and be slow to judge and quick to understand.

If someone has offended you, learn to forgive that person immediately so you won't become a prisoner to hate. We often think that if we do not forgive a person that we're harming them, but it's the opposite. The person who is taking the heavier blow is you. Forgiveness doesn't release the offender but the offended, and it doesn't mean that it lessens the hurt that was caused, but it loses the grip of resentment, allowing you to pull away and run toward freedom.

Write below:

1. Who have you not forgiven and why?
2. Are you willing to start the process of forgiveness and how will you go about doing it?
3. Are you ready to set the prisoner (you) free today?

_____

_____

_____

_____

_____

Scripture: Matthew 5:7: "Blessed are the merciful, for they shall receive mercy."

Cause and effects

For every cause, there's an effect. Good or bad.

Joining a gang is the cause and being shot seven times and confined to a wheelchair is the effect.

Choosing to change is the cause, and the effect is being where and who I am today. We must be wise in our decision-making, calculate our steps, and thoroughly consider the outcome. When we fail to do so, we become a gazelle wandering in a lion's territory, certain to be eaten.

1. What uncalculated decisions have you made that cost you greatly?
2. What steps will you take so you do not make the same mistakes?

_____

_____

_____

_____

_____

_____

_____

_____

_____

Scripture: Job 4:8: "As I have seen, those who plow iniquity and sow trouble reap the same."

The Streets Have No Heart

It's no secret that the streets have no heart. Just pay attention to the rap songs, the gang member telling his life story, ask the guy doing life in prison. The man laying in ICU, fighting for his life, or go visit a former gang member's grave. The signs and stories are everywhere. So why do we feel as though it'll be different for us somehow?

One day, I came into the house with blood all over my shirt and pants after being stabbed multiple times. My mom freaked out and rushed me to the ER after she sat there a while processing her emotions and coming down from being angry. Her words were, "Those guys you're hanging with are not your friends and those streets don't love you."

I thought to myself, *She has no clue of what she's talking about. We're living in a different time.*

After a while, I learned my mom was right.

The streets are unchanging and persistent in their pursuit to destroy. The streets are the same and will always be the same.

I've watched a friend get killed by his cousin over money, another friend got shot in his truck, and burned alive because of a robbery, another got shot during a fight, a cousin sentenced to life for murder, a brother sentenced to ten years in prison for drug charges, and another cousin who was to be drafted in the NBA lose his mind to drugs. I could go on and on about how the streets have destroyed so many because of pride. The streets are ruthless and have no hearts. It is controlled by Satan and his only agenda is to kill, steal, and destroy.

Write below:

1. Are you or someone you know involved in street life in any way?
2. Are you willing to get out or encourage someone to get out?
3. What are the steps you'll take to get out or encourage someone to get out?
4. Are you willing to accept or convey the truth about the dangers of the streets?

_____

_____

_____

_____

_____

_____

_____

_____

_____

_____

_____

Scripture: Deuteronomy 30:19: "This day I call the heavens and the earth as witnesses against you that I have set before you life and death, blessings and curses. Now choose life, so that you and your children may live."

Choosing God

We often hear it quoted, "I didn't choose the streets, it chose me." That sounds good to the person who wants to justify their behavior, but it's far from the truth. We all have a choice, even when our back is completely against the wall.

Consider Peter in the Bible. When he was asked if he was a follower of Jesus Christ, he denied that he was because he felt that his back was against the wall. Had he said yes, they would have tortured and killed him like they did Jesus. But fear of dying made him deny the life-giver. Same with most young men and women; we deny ourselves of a more peaceful and fruitful life because we fear that choosing the route of Christ will not bear fruit like the streets will. We settled for the illusion of happiness instead of accepting the joy that Christ gives.

Before choosing Christ, I was afraid that He wouldn't be to me all that Christians hyped Him up to be: a savior, redeemer, and a friend. I thought, *What good man would save, be a friend, or love someone like me?* When my back was up against the wall, I could have easily chosen to continue living a life of sin, but when asked if I accepted Jesus as my Lord and Savior, I said yes.

I was willing to take up my cross and be crucified with Him. And Jesus made good on His promise, He saved, redeemed, and is now my friend.

Write below:

1. Have you given God a chance to fully live through you? If so, how has it changed you? If you have not, why not?
2. Are you willing to go deeper in God, and how do you plan to do it?

_____

_____

_____

_____

_____

_____

_____

_____

_____

_____

_____

_____

_____

_____

Scripture: Psalm 119:30: "I have chosen the faithful way; I have placed Your ordinances before me."

Changing the Culture

As you all know, I grew up in a rough environment. I was given false ideas about life, God, and manhood. It wasn't until I began to challenge those beliefs that I was able to remove the veil and see the truth. Honestly, I had every reason to continue being who I once was. Abusive parents, absent father, my mother dying, being shot seven times, and more. I could have continued to play the victim, but I chose to be victorious.

My life is completely different than that of my parents. I'm here for my son; I encourage him instead of criticizing, I talk to him faster than I discipline him. I'm a loving and supportive husband. I lead in my home and in the world. I've chosen Christ instead of my own desires.

I was determined to change the culture in my home and be the man that I'd never seen modeled before me.

Changeling the culture not only gives you a fighting chance at life but also your children.

My son is much better of a boy than I was at his age because I am a better man. It's never too late to start reconditioning your mind and breaking bad habits. I challenge you to start now.

Write below:

1. Do you want to change the culture of how you might have been raised?
2. Are you willing to change the culture of your family, and how do you plan to do it?
3. Will you start today, instituting new behaviors and habits? Write what those new habits will be.

_____
_____
_____
_____
_____
_____
_____
_____
_____
_____
_____
_____

Scripture: Romans 12:2: "Do not be conformed to this world, but be transformed by the renewal of your mind, that by testing you may discern what is the will of God, what is good and acceptable and perfect."

Dare to be Different.

We live in a society where most are quick to conform and slow to be different. Many people are settling for a mundane lifestyle. Maybe it's the fear of failure, public opinion, fear of the unknown, or it's simply complacency. Whatever the reason may be, they are robbing themselves of a fruitful life.

I know this because I was once afraid to be bold and stand out. I was fearful and hid behind a life of complacency. I remember getting tired of the same routine. I would wake up, wash up, and go hang with my friends; I did that for almost ten years. Can you imagine how much I could have accomplished in that time? It wasn't until I chose to break free of the chains of conformity that I began to grow and evolve. My insecurities were replaced with confidence, fear with boldness, and a life of bitterness with the energy of joy.

Don't be afraid to step out from the 99% and be that 1% who dared to be different. The reward of the bold is glory, and the honor of the fearful is shame.

Write below:

1. Are you willing to be different, set apart, and accept what comes with being distinguished?
2. How do you plan to be different from those who are complacent?
3. Will you start today, and what will be your first step?

_____
_____
_____
_____
_____
_____
_____
_____
_____
_____
_____
_____
_____
_____
_____

Scripture: 1 Peter 2:9: *"But you are not like that, for you are a chosen people. You are royal priests, a holy nation, God's very own possession. As a result, you can show others the goodness of God, for he called you out of the darkness into his wonderful light."*

Anger

Anger has always been my resource for conflict resolution. It was the only tool I had to work with when having to fix a problem. I've always perceived anger as being strong. But it was only a dog standing guard at my fence to protect myself from being hurt and to hide my insecurities.

One day, I got into a fight with a guy who was much older and much bigger than me. I was so excited after winning, I ran down the street to tell my older cousin about the fight, and the words he'd spoken to me I'll never forget. He said, "Terrance, you responding to conflict with anger doesn't impress me. Aggression is all you've known since a child. Come and tell me when you are able to resolve a conflict in a peaceful manner, then I'll be impressed because that, little cousin, is your true strength."

Those words were like a dagger to my ego.

Anger is like untreated cancer; it will destroy you internally, causing sickness, stress, high blood pressure, anxiety, and fear until it kills you. You can choose to release anger's control over your life by identifying the lie, "That's just who I am," and replacing it with the truth, "For God has not given us a spirit of fear but of power, love, and self-control" (2 Timothy 1:7).

Today, I encourage you to choose peace and love, instead of anger. That is what impresses God.

Write below:

1. Are you willing to let go of anger and take hold of love?
2. If so, what will be your act of love today?
3. Who will you choose to love today?

_____

_____

_____

_____

_____

_____

_____

_____

_____

_____

_____

_____

_____

_____

_____

_____

_____
_____
_____
_____
_____
_____
_____
_____
_____
_____
_____
_____
_____
_____
_____

Take hold of God's love, and it will enable you to love.

> Scripture: Psalms 37: "Refrain from anger, and forsake wrath! Fret not yourself; it tends only to evil." "But you, O Lord, are a God merciful and gracious, slow to anger and abounding in steadfast love and faithfulness." "Whoever is slow to anger has great understanding, but he who has a hasty temper exalts folly."

RESOURCES

- National Grad Crisis Line. (877) 472-3457.
- National Sexual Assault Hotline. (800) 656-4673.
- Childhelp National Child Abuse Hotline. (800) 422-4453.
- CDC National HIV and AIDS Hotline. (800) 232-4636.
- Substance Abuse and Mental Health Services Administration National Helpline. (800) 662-4357.
- National Suicide Prevention Lifeline 1-800-273-TALK (8255)
- Crisis Text Line Text 741741
- National Domestic Violence Hotline1-800-799-SAFE (7233) or text "LOVEIS" to 22522
- Rape Abuse and Incest National Network (RAINN) 1-800-656-HOPE (4673)
- National Runaway Safeline 1-800-RUNAWAY (1-800-786-2929)

Facebook: @Terrance J. Pope

Instagram: terrance_j._pope

Website: http://transitionz7.com/

For Booking Contact:

Email: T7mentorship@gmail.com

Ph#: 313-918-6844

CPSIA information can be obtained
at www.ICGtesting.com
Printed in the USA
BVHW041330030422
632972BV00001B/1